40
HADITHS

Published by Tughra Books
335 Clifton Ave
Clifton, NJ 07011

www.tughrabooks.com

Edited by Ali Budak – Korkut Altay
Translated by Zainab Mahmoud
English text edited by Jane Louise Kandur – Makiz Ansari
Graphics and Layout İbrahim Akdağ

ISBN: 978-1-59784-208-2

40 HADITHS

TRANSLATION & COMMENTARY

Edited by
Ali Budak – Korkut Altay

TUGHRA
BOOKS

CONTENTS

A'udhu bi'izzatillahi wa qudratihi min sharri ma ajidu wa 'uhadhiru
("I seek refuge in God and His Power from the evil
that afflicts me and that which I fear.")

INTRODUCTION

Following Qur'an, the second most important authoritative source of Islamic knowledge is the Hadith. These enormous corpuses are the collection of the sayings and actions of Prophet Muhammad, peace be upon him. Through a sophisticated authentication process, a meticulous methodology and therefore a unique science of hadith collection which drew from reliable chains of narrators, was developed in order to capture the Prophet's direct quotes. This hadith literature has had a significant role in the formation of Islamic law and ethics. This volume follows suit the Prophet's encouraged tradition to focus on a select forty of his sayings rather then the entire collection. The ensuing discussion contains the original Arabic text, its English translation, and an edifying expansion of those pearls of wisdom.

Any translation is merely an indicative guideline to be followed; although the attempt is to use these guidelines in order to seek the essence of the text in question, nevertheless they can never be like the original manuscript. Those who have tried to seek the absolute meaning of the Qur'an through its translations have missed a great point and are in deception; for the true wonder and miracle of the Qur'an is in its very pristine revelation. Therefore, when translation is attempted the actual spirituality found in the original revelations and scripts of the Qur'an and for that matter the hadith[1] are minimised and at times even deprived.

---

[1] Sayings, actions and/or tacit approval of the Prophet Muhammad, peace and blessings be upon him.

This compilation is like a mere drop from the ocean of knowledge, a gleam of light from the reality and spirituality of the words of the holy Prophet. In this compilation of forty hadith great care has been taken to portray the meanings of those sublime words and contexts as closely to the original text as possible. Although the depths of meaning that encodes the Prophet's words of wisdom exceeds us in every dimension, it is necessary though to point out that experts in the field of hadith have been consulted in addition to our own independent research, nonetheless it is needless to mention that only the surface of this rich and vast universal light of words have been scratched.

We aspire to continue and relay the spirit from this fount of light into our lives, journeying with both the spirit and the intellect. In this quest for spirituality, all our prayers and endeavors are carried with the hope that they will be successful and accepted in His court of Mercy. We pray for forgiveness from the Creator for any unintended deficiency in our work.

NOTE: *The translations and commentary of the hadith are a collection from the various books of M. Fethullah Gülen.*

ABOUT THE EDITORS:

Ali Budak holds a PhD in Hadith. He is a staff editor at Işık Yayınları, a leading publisher in Turkey, and a frequent speaker and writer on Islam's hadith tradition. He is the author of five books, including Fasting in Islam.

Korkut Altay is a staff editor at Tughra Books and translator of various books into English, including Topkapı Palace: Milestones in Ottoman History, The Museum of Turkish and Islamic Arts.

عَنِ ابْنِ عُمَرَ قَالَ قَالَ رَسُولُ اللهِ صَلَّى اللهُ عَلَيْهِ وَسَلَّمَ:
اَلْمُؤْمِنُ الَّذِي يُخَالِطُ النَّاسَ وَيَصْبِرُ عَلَى أَذَاهُمْ أَعْظَمُ أَجْرًا مِنَ الْمُؤْمِنِ
الَّذِي لَا يُخَالِطُ النَّاسَ وَلَا يَصْبِرُ عَلَى أَذَاهُمْ

UNITY WITH GOD WHILE AMONG OTHERS

"The believer who mixes with people and bears the troubles they cause has greater reward than the one who does not."

(Ibn Maja, Fitan, 23; Tirmidhi, Qiyama, 55)

This world has a few different faces; one of them is the material or "worldly" face, which is transitory. It throws at us a hundred blows in return for a small bounty. This transitory aspect of the world is a diversion, a deceit. It is this transitory face of world that is sought after and adored by those who solely run after worldly concerns; a believer is expected to be well aware of this hideous face behind the mask.

We are supposed to form a sense of balance between this world and the Hereafter by keeping this perspective in mind; we need to remember that the world is transitional while the Hereafter is eternal. The Prophet never turned his back on this world, yet he was also with the Creator at all times, even in the midst of crowd.

We can see this in the hadith we have mentioned at the beginning. This is how humans should approach others; if they do, then rivers of peace will flow where once there were heaps of false words and actions. Just like how teachers with their students are patient with regards to some of the spiritual hardships and difficulties faced; and demonstrate great self–sacrifice.

Devotion to spiritual prosperity means finding the path to true wisdom and piety, and this in turn will result in affection and closeness with the Creator. This path of true guidance will become our way of life; our only aim in the world will be to convey and represent the sublime realities of faith and to behave with great devotion, just like the Prophet did when he chose not to be captivated by the attractions of Paradise during the Ascension and returned to his followers.

Those with true awareness of the passing attractions that this life offers will never be deceived or become captivated by the transience and negative aspects of the universe. They will remain within their communities with a constant spiritual connection with the Creator.

Throughout his life the Prophet never considered the offers of the world; his arrival in the world was no different to his departure... he was wrapped in a cloth and placed in a crib on his arrival and he departed from this world again wrapped in a shroud.

The Prophet spent his lifetime striving to establish a balance between this world and the Hereafter and to convey faith, spirituality and the universal principles through his teachings, to many civilizations without any concessions. Never deceived by the pleasures of the universe, he lived in total peace and confidence, submitting his soul and his all to God. Prophet Muhammad, peace and blessings be upon him, departed after having devoted his entire life to the rescue of humankind and for the gain of His Creator's pleasure.

One day Umar ibn al-Khattab[2] entered the home of bliss and saw the holy Prophet lying on a straw mat; he began to weep with a deep sense of care. When the Prophet asked why he was crying Umar replied: *"While Caesar and Chosroes live a life of luxury, you are the Messenger of God and you live in such destitution."* The Prophet explained in a way that will always remain in the minds and hearts of all: *"Don't you agree that the luxuries of the world should be theirs, and that those of the Hereafter should be ours?"*

The Prophet never neglected the beauties of the world; he was fully aware and appreciative of the wisdom of the creation within the universe and he portrayed this to others. He strove alongside his Compan-

---

[2]   One of the holy Prophet's closest companions and also later one of the first four Caliphs

ions to transmit such manifest beauties and the realities of life through Islamic teachings to the entire world. Thus, considering all his achievements over a period that only spans twenty-three years, we can confidently claim that his message and practice have provided a breakthrough in the overall progress of humanity since ancient times.

Once again, it is necessary to repeat that the holy Prophet never neglected or underestimated the life of this world; he knew the limits as to its value and importance. From the believer's standpoint, there is the positive face of the world, like the fertile ground, which views the world as bedrock wherein the good seeds for the hereafter can be grown. It was this value and significance that the holy Prophet guided his followers towards.

The human person's willpower is directly proportional to the level of patience they have. Patience is the muscle of resistance and tolerance given to humanity, a great virtue that brings forth a hidden spiritual strength from within. There are innumerable doses of wisdom, prophetic, saintly and scholarly legacies and countless reasons for why and how patience can be the means to reach perfection and to progress in life as a conscious and genuine member of a community.

The first aspect of patience is steadfastness in worship. The second and most important aspect of patience, particularly for youth is to have patience against defiance and malice. This kind of patience is the greatest way to protect oneself, especially in contemporary times where indecency, vice and corruption are continuously on the rise. This form of patience is the second stepping stone towards human spiritual development, a great way toward the peak of one's given potential.

The third form of patience can be arguably the greatest of all; that during the times of disaster or grave troubles, times which God has sent for many universal and comprehensive points of wisdom the particular focus to awaken one's resignation to Divine decree.

The fourth aspect is patience against the pomp and vanities of this world which can strongly appeal to the carnal self. Once again the practice of which can be a means of dramatic spiritual growth.

The fifth facet is to show diligence and leave aside all kinds of material and for that matter even spiritual expectations and or rewards for the sake of His Glory. This level of fervent love and quest for pleasing the Almighty can only be achieved and for that matter attempted by those who have reached a level of deep maturity in their faith.

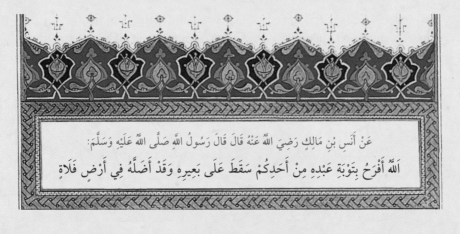

عَنْ أَنَسِ بْنِ مَالِكٍ رَضِيَ اللهُ عَنْهُ قَالَ قَالَ رَسُولُ اللهِ صَلَّى اللهُ عَلَيْهِ وَسَلَّمَ:
اَللهُ أَفْرَحُ بِتَوْبَةِ عَبْدِهِ مِنْ أَحَدِكُمْ سَقَطَ عَلَى بَعِيرِهِ وَقَدْ أَضَلَّهُ فِي أَرْضٍ فَلَاةٍ

DIVINE PLEASURE WITH REPENTANCE

"God is more pleased with the repentance of His servant than any
of you feels joy for finding the camel that he has lost in the desert."

(Bukhari, Da'awat, 4; Muslim, Tawba, 1, 7)

This hadith is narrated in another way meaning that God is more
pleased with the repentance of a servant when he turns towards
Him (for repentance) than the one among you who rides his camel into a waterless desert, where the camel carries both his food and drink, and the camel strays; having lost all hope of its return, one lies down in the shadows, disappointed about his camel. When he awakes he finds the camel standing before him. He takes hold of his nose string and out of boundless joy says: *"O Lord, you are my servant and I am your Lord."* He commits this mistake out of extreme delight. God's delight upon His servant's repentance is more than such a man's (Muslim, Tirmidhi, Ibn Maja).

Repentance is a means of deliverance; it is turning to the Creator in regret for an error or a sin committed, for straying from the path. It is this that the Prophet is referring to in the above hadith. Of course, the word pleasure should not be attributed or ascribed to the Creator in the same way that we understand it; the pleasure of the Divine is so intense and absolute, it is a pleasure of such sacredness, that humans can never imagine it or even begin

4

to understand it. The most important fact is that we acknowledge to a degree the extent of Divine pleasure and happiness for our repentance.

There are two aspects of repentance; firstly, there is the perspective that looks towards humans and their intention to reform, spurred on by a continuous sense of regret. The second aspect looks to the role of the Creator, His forgiveness and the great compassion by which he opens the doors, saying *"O, My servants, I have neither forgotten nor deserted you, and every time you remember Me and ask for My forgiveness, even if you break your promise fifty times, know that I am here."*

The Prophet said: *"God forgives those who repent."*[3] Repentance means turning towards the Most Merciful and begging for his forgiveness; obtaining God's forgiveness means reopening the doors and paths towards His compassion. When someone disobeys God, all the doors and paths which lead to Him are blocked, but when deep regret is felt deep within, when they self-critique their actions, intentions and to their own selves say: *"Why did I take that path which opposes both my nature and my belief?"* This eventually turns into an effort to make amends, a self-correction; it is at this time that the doors and the paths that lead to Divine Compassion begin to reopen. Whatever mistakes we make in our life we should ask for forgiveness from the Creator and recite this supplication, for God is the Most Compassionate, the Merciful: *"O Most Compassionate, Forgiver of all, have mercy on us and forgive our sins, and protect us from evil."*

Another important point of repentance is that, it is usually modified by the adjective *nasuh*—literally meaning pure, sincere, reforming, improving, and repairing. *Tawba nasuh* expresses a benevolent criticism, and that one is giving counsel to his or her *nafs* (self). *Nasuh* comes from the same root with *nasiha* (guidance). *Nasiha* denotes that a person thinks well, sees well, and wants good for others. "Religion is guidance" which actually means wishing others true wellness; this entails directing them towards the True Path, taking their hand and guiding them, informing them about the realities of life, the need for seeking a point of recourse and recognizing God Almighty, to understand and come to know His selected and fine Messenger, and the wonders, richness and euphoria that is generated by faith.

---

[3]   The literal translation of the original text is "God turns to those who turn to Him," since *tawba* (repentance), means turning to God in Arabic.

A person's greatest goal for their benevolence must be their own soul, for protecting one's life is one of the five essentials to be protected by Islamic law (ie. one's religion, intellect, life, property, and dignity). A human is responsible for refraining from drinking alcohol, committing adultery, blasphemy and straying from the Divine Path; all of these prohibitions are related to one of the five essentials mentioned. Every human must protect both their soul and ego from inclining to evil, from becoming the fuel that enflames hell; every person must know the fate of their soul and the consequences of living a life of ignorance.

In Qur'an, people who are aware of such matters yet continue to overindulge and persist in the pursuit of their personal pleasures through such acts irrespective, are referred to as "Fuel for the hellfire." That is, every human being has the duty to display kindness and benevolence to their own ego and every one is responsible for protecting themselves against sin or evil; in fact, we need to show such kindness to ours souls that: *"When God saves you from disbelief and straying from the Path of Truth, the mere thought of repeating the same mistake will be as painful as the thought of going to hell."*

Unfortunately, there is always the possibility that a believing person may still fall to error as the human tendency to progress and for that matter to regress is limitless.. It is at this time that a believer must motivate their mind and conscience by thinking: *"I am in this situation of inner suffocation, unease and emptiness because I have ignored the commands of my Designer and my only salvation is to obey His orders."* The way to rebuild and strengthen one's relationship with one's Creator is to make a genuine concerted effort and being sincere in repentance.

Another point that needs to be considered is that a conception of goodness in a person's soul will prevent them from reenacting previous sins and mistakes. A human must desire to be a good person; they must want their family and children to be good individuals, and kind and respectable people of the community. A believer must always have the desire to become a better human. They must be determined and devoted, and this will help prevent them falling into grave errors; the mere thought of evil or sin should be considered an offense. The path that leads one away from the Creator in turn will encourage them to consider the consequences and hopefully lead one to repentance.

In Qur'an God informs us: *"O you who believe! Turn to God in sincere and reforming repentance"* (Tahrim 66:8). Sincere repentance means having found the truth and faith and having reached a point of distinction between good and evil, with faith in and dependence on the Creator. So, if regardless of all your attempts and efforts to avoid evil, you do unfortunately stray from the Divine Path, you should never consider yourself a lost cause, because the Most Merciful One, is the All-Forgiver, with the exception of associating partners with God[4] (Nisa 4:48).

Thus, there is no reason to be oppressed by evil; there is always a door or a path of light to follow. One can turn to the Creator and ask for His forgiveness, show sincere repentance by turning one self and one's life towards guidance. Naturally there are some conditions that need to be fulfilled to be truly repentant before God:

The first: If the sin involved the rights of another human, the sinner must ask forgiveness from the other party before asking for forgiveness from God.

The second: The sinner must be sincere and determined not to repeat the same sin again.

The third: A sinner should repent as soon as they possibly can; there should be no opportunity to sin again between the act and the person's repentance.

Another aspect of repentance is that: Sin or evil should give the soul a feeling of fear and disgust; this is in a sense the punishment inflicted by a person's conscience. The repentance of those who become accustomed to evil, those who have no concept of punishment or guilt for sins, will be just the utterance of certain words of repentance.

True repentance is the feeling of remorse and remorse is a human emotion, it is guilt felt deep within the soul. Then the words of repentance become the voice of the heart. The expressions of Prophet Muhammad, peace and blessings be upon him, used in this hadith show us the importance of remorse: *"I repent and seek forgiveness from You. O Lord I am your helpless servant*

---

4   For associating partners with God or to deny Him is a crime of universal proportion. If Creator is not regarded, there will truly be no regard for His creation and the value of the *art* therefore will grossly be abused, if the *Artist* is not acknowledged rightly. As a result, such denial is worse then thousands of lies with repercussions also at the universal level and therefore an act unforgiveable.

with no ability to live or die except on Your command. I ask for Your forgiveness for my sins." This example of repentance was reported in another hadith.

After performing one's prayers a person who repents for their sins should prostrate and recite sincere supplications, saying things like: "*O God! Inspire me with guidance and protect me from the mischief of my soul.*" Another prayer of forgiveness, known as "*sayyid al-istighfar*"[5] is: "*O God: You are my Lord. There is no God but You. You created me and I am Your servant. I follow Your covenant and pledge to the best of my ability. I seek refuge in You from the evils that I have committed. I acknowledge the bounties You have sent upon me and I confess to my sins. Forgive me for no one can forgive sins except You.*"

These supplications, if recited from the depths of the soul, are a form of sincere repentance. Although they are not included in the hadith, some believers from earlier periods additionally said "Ya Ghaffar," "Ya Ghafur"; it is also good to seek refuge in Him through these two names from Asma al-Husna related to His forgiving the sins and mistakes of His servants.

Repentance occurs when we feel remorse and our souls are distressed; our prayers of repentance are accepted when we express words of sincere remorse. A human being may ask for forgiveness for sins they have committed, but if their heart and mind are not in keeping with the words of repentance, if there is no true feeling of guilt or remorse in the soul, then this display of regret is in vain. A person must at the least have a sense of regret in their heart and this regret should be portrayed in words of remorse that emanate deep from the soul. Repentance is not merely for show or some kind of ceremony to convey one's remorse to others; it is literally standing before the Creator and admitting our sins with great regret and emotion, asking for compassion and forgiveness from the Merciful One.

5   For the original text of the prayer, see *Selected Prayers of Prophet Muhammad and Great Muslim Saints*, The Light, Inc., New Jersey: 2006 (p.10).

عَنْ عُمَرَ بْنِ الْخَطَّابِ أَنَّهُ قَالَ:

قَدِمَ عَلَى رَسُولِ اللَّهِ صَلَّى اللَّهُ عَلَيْهِ وَسَلَّمَ بِسَبْيٍ فَإِذَا امْرَأَةٌ مِنَ السَّبْيِ تَبْتَغِي
إِذَا وَجَدَتْ صَبِيًّا فِي السَّبْيِ أَخَذَتْهُ فَأَلْصَقَتْهُ بِبَطْنِهَا وَأَرْضَعَتْهُ فَقَالَ لَنَا رَسُولُ
اللَّهِ صَلَّى اللَّهُ عَلَيْهِ وَسَلَّمَ: أَتَرَوْنَ هَذِهِ الْمَرْأَةَ طَارِحَةً وَلَدَهَا فِي النَّارِ قُلْنَا
لَا وَاللَّهِ وَهِيَ تَقْدِرُ عَلَى أَنْ لَا تَطْرَحَهُ فَقَالَ رَسُولُ اللَّهِ صَلَّى اللَّهُ عَلَيْهِ وَسَلَّمَ
لَلَّهُ أَرْحَمُ بِعِبَادِهِ مِنْ هَذِهِ بِوَلَدِهَا

THE COMPASSION OF THE COMPASSIONATE ONE

"(Once) captives were brought in front the Prophet. Among them was a woman. The woman, longing for her child, ran back and forth, picking up every child she saw, pressing them to her breast to nurse them. Indicating this woman, the Prophet asked, 'Do you think this woman would throw her child (she has pressed to her breast) into a fire?' (The Companions) said, 'No! This merciful woman would never throw her child into the fire!' The Prophet then said, 'God is more merciful to His servants than this woman is to her child.'"

(Bukhari, Adab, 18; Muslim, Tawba, 22)

9

E very Muslim must seriously consider this hadith, act accordingly and be more tolerant towards others. This does not mean that we should display exaggerated compassion or even attempt to reach the compassion of God; rather, it means that we must consider compassion from the angle of the general principles of the Prophet's life and the hadith Qudsi: *"My mercy has surpassed my wrath."*

Another important aspect is how this subject reflects on us: As a nation we have not made enough efforts to demonstrate the realities and truth to the youth of today. By neglecting our own youth and our duties we have also failed to portray a message that is more important than air or water to the young people of the world.

Comparing ourselves to the Companions, who were also responsible for conveying the truth, just as we are, and the great efforts they made to convey these words of truth to every corner of the earth, we can clearly see just how lazy and idle a nation we have become. The Companions searched day and night to find those who had a desire to learn the truth in their souls; and the conveying of Islam became their way of life.

Thus, believers have to ask themselves this question: have we performed our duty in sharing the beauties of Mercy and Compassion that we benefit from? And if the answer to this question is no, then we have to answer for so much. We must make the compassion of God our direction and having well internalized and understood the meaning of compassion as the Compassionate One displays, we need to reflect through our characters such affection that the Compassionate One shows to us and the entire universe; we should both use and heed the lesson from this example in order to fulfill the duties we have both to others and to our principles.

عَنْ عَبْدِ اللهِ بْنِ مَسْعُودٍ قَالَ:

نَامَ رَسُولُ اللهِ صَلَّى اللهُ عَلَيْهِ وَسَلَّمَ عَلَى حَصِيرٍ فَقَامَ وَقَدْ أَثَّرَ فِي جَنْبِهِ فَقُلْنَا يَا رَسُولَ اللهِ لَوِ اتَّخَذْنَا لَكَ وِطَاءً فَقَالَ مَا لِي وَمَا لِلدُّنْيَا مَا أَنَا فِي الدُّنْيَا إِلَّا كَرَاكِبٍ اسْتَظَلَّ تَحْتَ شَجَرَةٍ ثُمَّ رَاحَ وَتَرَكَهَا

④

A HUMAN IS A TRAVELER AND THE
UNIVERSE HIS SHADE

"The messenger of God had been sleeping on a straw mat. When he woke up the mat had left marks on his body. We said to him, 'O, Messenger of God! Let us prepare a soft bed for you.' The Prophet of God replied, 'I have got nothing to do with the world. I am like a traveler in this world, who sits under a tree for its shade, then leaves it."

(Tirmidhi, Zuhd, 44)

What is the universe? How should we form a balance between the temporary and mortal things of this world? Why have human beings been sent to this world and where are we heading? These topics, which are frequently questioned by philosophers and which have been discussed for centuries, were clearly and concisely answered by Prophet Muhammad.

It was reported by Ibn Umar that the Prophet said: *"Live in the world as if you were a stranger or be like a traveler. Regard yourself as one of the residents of the grave (before you die)!"* (Tirmidhi, Zuhd, 25).

This hadith, which is so meaningful and to the point, is a description of *taqwa* or piety; that is, we should disregard worldly pleasures and maintain a balance in our lives between the universe and the Hereafter.

After all humans are destitute in this world; as Rumi said: *"A human is like a reed that has been torn from its bed to make a flute. It constantly moans because it has been removed from its True Owner and this moaning continues throughout its life."*

A human is a traveler and our journey, which begins with the spiritual creation, continues with the journey of the womb, birth, childhood, adolescence, old age, the grave and then terminates in Paradise or Hell. How aware are we of this journey? If a person truly sees themselves as a traveler in this world they will carry on their journey without being caught up in the various pleasures that do nothing but slow them down on this long and sometimes difficult journey of life.

Regarding oneself as already dead means that we cannot be rescued or protected from the deceit of Satan until we are aware of death in our daily lives. A person should die in terms of their carnal self and worldly desires, if their spirituality and conscience are to be revived. Those who attribute everything to materialism have in fact been caught up in the misery of fleeting worldly pleasures.

Therefore, we should take into consideration some of the aspects of human existence as a traveler in this world: God, the Owner of all on the earth has provided humankind with what we need both in this world and the Hereafter; however, due to our ignorance, we sacrifice these means entirely in this physical world. The correct approach is to use a small percentage for the benefits of the physical world, with the remaining portion being used for preparation for the Hereafter.

O people! God the Merciful One has blessed you with provisions in the womb, throughout your childhood and will continue blessing you with these provisions when you become feeble in old age until the time of your death. O people! Also know that you will face great difficulties, which will force you to be cautious and aware. These are as follows:

1. The first is the separation of death which removes human beings from the earth and from their loved ones.
2. The second is the feared journey to the universe of eternity.
3. Our lifespan may be short, but the journey it entails is long and tiring; with no provisions left for this journey a feeling of weakness and helplessness, of being subjected to distress and suffering will overwhelm us.

So why are humans so heedless and ignorant? Many try to avoid or ignore the fact that God knows and sees all, like an ostrich that sticks its head into the sand in the hope that no one will see him; but how long will you keep crediting the fleeting things of this physical world and be heedless of the permanent truths of the eternal life?

عَنْ أَبِي سَعِيدٍ الْخُدْرِيِّ قَالَ سَمِعْتُ رَسُولَ اللهِ صَلَّى اللهُ عَلَيْهِ وَسَلَّمَ يَقُولُ:
مَنْ رَأَى مِنْكُمْ مُنْكَرًا فَلْيُغَيِّرْهُ بِيَدِهِ فَإِنْ لَمْ يَسْتَطِعْ فَبِلِسَانِهِ
فَإِنْ لَمْ يَسْتَطِعْ فَبِقَلْبِهِ وَذَلِكَ أَضْعَفُ الْإِيمَانِ

(5)

WAYS OF CHANGING EVIL

"Whosoever of you sees an evil (act), let him change it with his hand; if he is not able to do so, then (let him change it) with his tongue; if he is not able to do so, then with his heart - and that is the weakest of faith."

(Muslim, Iman, 78)

If any form of evil which is undesirable in Islam is seen, then physical attempt needs to be made to change the situation, however if the physical attempt is not possible, then the case in question needs to be verbally nullified, and with composure and calmness the evil aspects of the matter needs to be articulated or some kind of advice to transform the situation needs to be made. If for the believer this approach is also unsuccessful or not possible due to unsuitable conditions then the discomfort from the evil act needs to be felt and made obvious with the heart and one's ac-

14

tions, and this latter is the weakest of ways to change an evil act, the weakest demonstration of faith.

Let us think of an evil act, which acts like a disease that eats away and eventually destroys the fabric of society; for instance adultery, drugs, usury or profiteering. Malicious beings and the enemies of a nation thrive freely on such diseases; the consequences of the above-mentioned evil acts are well-known and widely understood by most members of society.

Given the society is mainly a Muslim society, one may think that perhaps *there is nothing one can do*, since reliance on the government to protect and enforce law and to eliminate the source of such evils, is given. As it happened, under the Islamic rule, the leaders would actually intervene with law enforcement capacity in order to prevent acts of evil from their negative social effects and manifestations. Such was the physical form of prevention and elimination of evil.

Unfortunately in our contemporary times, there is neither action against nor prevention from these diseases; even worse is the lack of encouragement for kindness and good actions amongst people. If, for instance, one watch someone in the street engaged in a foul act deplorable by religion and therefore attempted to intervene, it is likely that the response maybe violent. It is best therefore to reserve physical intervention to the authorities and law enforcement agencies.

If physical intervention is not possible, then persuasion or words of caution can be the next step. Given the government does not take into consideration, let alone complies with the principles of God as a part of society's laws, or given that the law enforcement agencies are weak to implement laws and as result unable to prevent iniquity from society, or in worse case scenario if the government even allows such acts to take place; then according to the stated Hadith, it is incumbent on the members of society to endeavor for its prevention.

To take as an example, if adultery, alcohol or usury are prevalent under a particular system or form of law and physical intervention to prevent it is impossible, then one's duty is to endeavor and transform it by persuasion with composure and calm so that the reason and consequences of the malice is understood. For instance usury is a disease that destroys society's viability, that adultery is a form of cancer that eats away the dignity of a nation. Well received persuasion can then be an effective approach.

15

One's duty is to encourage and instigate within the offenders the realization for the harm that these evil actions entail and for them to abhor, fear and eventually abandon such ethically offensive practices. Most of us are fortunate to live in a time when freedom to express and explain the harm and pitfalls that follows every evil practices; this may not be the case at certain periods or in certain places in the world, be it in predominantly Muslim countries or other parts of the world.

There have been such periods—which can potentially return—wherein one is prohibited to even utter a word against widespread transgressions. In those periods, if one was to for instance, speak against *"interest and alcohol as diseases that will ruin our lives, so we must find a solution,"* one can be accused of attempting to instill religious laws into the legal, economic or political system.

If one is unable to even speak out, then the only alternative left would be to express oneself and clear one's conscience with strong feelings of disapproval within one's heart and consequently avoid such situations and such people; this would be the faintest of all forms of prevention or action though; having said that, it is important to be aware of the kind of company one is with. To remain in the company of an offender can potentially desensitize one towards the offence, possibly leading to the acceptance of such acts as the norm of daily life. This would lead to the gradual downfall of individuals and/or communities. For example, those who have a relationship or friendship with a person who commits adultery may start to view the iniquity as a normal. This could even lead to a Divine punishment that may afflict the entire community.

In spite of all this, there is also a positive aspect that can be considered. While grave ethical and moral transgressions can take place within a nation, if however there is an active and spiritually dynamic group within the same nation, serving for noble purposes, then for these blessed people's sake, God will save the entire community from disasters and their function becomes like a spiritual lightning rod.

On the contrary though if a society is deprived of such people, of those individuals whose proactive initiative in transforming malpractices from society is absent, then those societies become readily susceptible to disasters and potentially are destroyed.

This is why a believer should avoid very intimate relationships with those who consciously participate in immoral acts. Following suit the Prophetic tradition of forming warm and positive relationships with people from all kinds of backgrounds, it has become a duty upon Muslims to build relationships with individuals from all walks of life. Like everything else, one's intentions and acting within certain parameters of conduct are noteworthy. For the main purpose should be to share the beauties that the spiritual tradition of Islam offers and hopefully become that trigger to awaken within them purposes higher and beyond indulgences, offences and foul actions. If the pursuit is Divine pleasure then such relationship will be recorded as meritorious deed.

Undoubtedly, the mere dislike for those who participate in morally illegitimate deeds, for those who have no regard for the Creator and as a consequence for the creation, and for those who are a dangerous threat to this world is the weakest form of faith, but being the means to awaken within such people the true aim of life, of sublime purposes for human existence with persuasive and genuine manner becomes a duty incumbent on all. Prophet Muhammad, peace and blessings be upon him, said: *"I have been commanded to fulfill my duties and guide mankind."* The Prophet was sent by God to be that shining guide to his community on one hand and on the other to fulfill his duties before the Creator as His appointed messenger.

Based on such a meticulous precedent of exalted mannerism and etiquette of serving humankind, our duty therefore is to approach everyone with regard, calm and beautiful mannerism, so that through such genuine conduct, the transformative capacity for human goodness can be activated and the elegance of faith can wake within their souls. This way of no anger, resentment or harshness, can then demonstrate the reality and splendor of Islam.

This was the reason why God told Moses and Aaron *"Go, both of you, to Pharaoh, Speak to him mildly,"* (Taha 20:43-44) urging them to approach Pharaoh in a friendly manner so the truth in what they had to say would be portrayed with effect and their guidance would not be in vain.

Based on such prophetic precedents of exalted mannerism and gentle approaches, all our communications and forming relationships should also reflect that kind of integrity, for if the approach is for the sake of the Exalted One and is to relay the Divine principles, any relative difficulties which may entail can become endurable. Dislike towards deplorable actions of others for the sake of God should not go to the level of hatred of the human person.

عَنْ عُبَادَةَ بْنِ الصَّامِتِ عَنِ النَّبِيِّ صَلَّى اللهُ عَلَيْهِ وَسَلَّمَ قَالَ:

رُؤْيَا الْمُؤْمِنِ جُزْءٌ مِنْ سِتَّةٍ وَأَرْبَعِينَ جُزْءًا مِنَ النُّبُوَّةِ

6

DREAMS

"Dreams of a believer are one forty sixth part of prophethood"

(Bukhari, Ta'bir, 26; Muslim, Ru'ya, 6)

From this it can be understood that prophethood consists of forty-six depths, forty-six parts, provides forty-six meanings, and has forty-six principles. Scholars have interpreted this in connection with the dreams that Prophet Muhammad peace and blessings be upon him, began to have related to what was his forthcoming mission, for six months before he was blessed with the prophethood.

According to a report in Sahih al-Bukhari,[6] the Prophet would have dreams at the break of dawn and these dreams would actually happen the next day; and this continued on for six months while he was married to Khadija. He began to have these dreams or would have certain visions on Mount Hira, and this was to be the prelude to his mission. When these dreams ended the revelations began. The total period of Prophet Mu-

---

6   The most reliable collection of Hadith.

hammad's, peace and blessings be upon him, prophethood continued for twenty-three years, if each year was to be divided into two and the first six months was included as one part of the prophethood, then these dreams that occurred before the onset of revelation can be considered one of the forty-six parts of prophethood.

The holy Prophet also described dreams as *"the greatest truth approaching the last day."* But why would this be the case? Prophethood, the truth behind the dreams or visions, came to an end with the final Prophet, and therefore the possibility to physically see or receive advice from the Prophet is not there. Great personalities with true wisdom like Imam Rabbani, Imam Shazuli, Abdulqadr Jilani, Ahmad Rufai or Bediüzzaman Said Nursi, have all departed from this world; leaving behind the communities of us mortal human beings, whose knowledge in relation to true understanding of spiritual values, is quite minimum, if at all. Time cannot be winded back in order to reach out or benefit from the Prophetic visions nor is possible to physically see the Prophets of this universe of truth.

What can afford a level of comfort for this separation is this Hadith about dreams and also what the great Junayd Baghdadi reported as saying; *"I spoke to the Prophet in my dream; he spoke to me and gave me these orders...."* To be able to communicate with the Prophet is an honor, of which we are deprived, nevertheless amidst the grave lack in spiritual consciousness, despite the prevalence of malice and disorder, the Merciful One with His compassion bless us with messages of wisdom through dreams, and through the pious souls of others, even more preciously blesses us with seeing the Prophet, his virtuous Companions and other great and holy spiritual people who submitted themselves to God. This is why the Prophet said *"The greatest truth nearing the last day is dreams."* These dreams were referred to by the Prophet as *mubasharat* - visions of glad tidings.

This great manifestation of compassion must be a form of encouragement for believers during these times when humans over-indulge in worldly pleasures and heed the desires of their egos; without such Divine encouragement, life in the world would be a continuous uphill struggle.

Although dreams are a fact of life, a natural occurrence, nevertheless a believer must know how the extent of its reliability. Everything has a measured dose and thereby balance. For example, it is well-known that the brain uses glucose, but if there was over-indulgence of sugar, serious health problems will surface overtime. Dreams are no different. If we rely on dreams too much in the quest of discerning their meanings and begin to introduce them in our daily lives then life will be based on dreams, and no escape to the reality of the world.

Dreams, unlike the Qur'an and hadith, are not an authoritative source of knowledge to base our judgments upon; giving priority to dreams and visions instead of basic sources of religion or trying to make use of the jinn and devils is dangerous. Ghulam Ahmad was among those who lost when he tried to prove that he was gifted with spiritual powers. He began a six-month hunger strike to prove the superiority of Islam to his Buddhists and Hindu Brahmans contemporaries; was this way to convey Islam? Consequently Ghulam Ahmad first claimed that he was the Mahdi or Guided One, and he then went on to claim that he was the awaited leader followed by his claim to be a prophet; his greatest downfall was when he claimed to be "God."

This is just one of the ways in which the Devil uses evil-spirits to deceive humans. Acting upon dreams, relying on visions and spirits all begin with a sense of innocence, it can engulf the person so much so that before they realize that they deserted the true path of faith.

The core of the matter is to take responsibility to follow Qur'an and the Sunna[7] of the Prophet. For instance, even if you ascend to the sky, meet God's Messenger by transcending time, or witness various manifestations from God, all of these mean nothing in comparison to carrying out the Sunna of the Prophet properly.

Instead of wishing to be seen as a saintly figure, a good Muslim should seek to be "an ordinary person among people." When those around him said to Umar, "You have pleased the Prophet and Abu Bakr; you shall be in Paradise and your pavilion will be the heavens," he just looked at them with a bitter smile and said "I will be pleased if I can leave the world as I came." This is how those with true understanding of faith should think.

If we live according to the Qur'an and the Sunna and embed the principles and regulations of true faith in our lives, then God will bless us in a similar way as He has blessed those with wisdom. For real benefit comes from nothing else then faith and religion; if dreams provide positive motivation, we should draw this much out of it.

---

[7] The practice and tacit approvals of Prophet Muhammad, peace and blessings be upon him.

عَنْ جَابِرٍ رَضِيَ اللَّهُ عَنْهُ قَالَ قَالَ رَسُولُ اللَّهِ صَلَّى اللَّهُ عَلَيْهِ وَسَلَّمَ:

أَخْشَى مَا خَشِيتُ عَلَى أُمَّتِي كِبَرُ الْبَطْنِ، وَمُدَاوَمَةُ النَّوْمِ وَالْكَسَلُ وَضَعْفُ الْيَقِينِ

⑦

OBESITY, EXCESSIVE SLEEP, LAZINESS AND
WEAKNESS OF FAITH

*What I fear for my followers is a large stomach, excessive
sleep, idleness and lack of certainty (in faith)."*

(Kanz al-Ummal, 3:460)

First, let us take a brief look at the subject and content of this hadith, a matter that caused the Prophet of God great concern, we
will then continue to examine the connections between the subjects within the hadith.

A large stomach is written in the original hadith as *kibar al- batn;* referring to those who overindulge in eating and drinking, whose lives are sur-

21

rounded by food consumption, with their only goal in life to indulge in the pleasures of this world. As a result and unnecessarily their bodies are over burdened with excessive weight. Such people are those for whom the Prophet feared most.

Excessive sleep is another potential threat to be feared. The average sleep human adults need is five hours a day. Some physicians state that exceeding these five hours can have serious repercussions on the body. This is a subject that many scholars, including Imam Ghazzali and Bediuzzaman Said Nursi, elucidated on the dangers that excessive sleep entails especially in respect to the relationship between the created and the Creator. In the past, people in *madrasa* circles and dervish lodges would attempt to implement a discipline of three hours sleep every night.

Hence, from this aspect, "excessive sleep" is expressed as *iz'af* which means excess. There is sufficient awareness from both doctors and scholars to know the five hour requirement of the human body for sleep. Effort should be made to reduce long sleeping hours down to the required amount. Once the body has become familiarized with this amount, the hours can even be further reduced.

But it is noteworthy to highlight that those who eat excessively and have very little to nil will power to discipline their eating or drinking habits will never be able to reduce or change their sleeping patterns. This is a subject to which we will return when the connection between the subjects as a whole is examined.

Idleness is a grave condition to be in. One of those persistent issues that the Prophet would always seek refuge in God from was idleness. At the heart of Islamic philosophy lies dynamism and motion which is manifest in every part and every layer of the universe. Islam intervened in anything that was contrary to this philosophy of dynamism; in other words Qur'anic worldview tried to recharge any inaction to constructive and beneficial actions. For instance, land that was left uncultivated and idle was distributed under the condition that it be revived and cultivated. It compelled the saved and idle wealth which had not been circulated through business or trade, as a serious spiritual threat to the rich, and this is why idle wealth is also included in the money from which *zakat* is calculated.

Islam's viewpoint towards indolence and those idle people who because of their lack of concert earn their living through begging is no different than its conception of idle wealth or idle land; on the contrary, it is even more intolerable. The fact that this subject is mentioned in the hadith as one of the Prophet's greatest fears for his followers is due to the human tendency towards idle behavior.

Lack of certainty in faith is one of the gravest of matters to be feared from. There are different degrees of certainty; first, that which comes from knowledge (*ilm al-yaqin*); second, which depends on seeing and observation (*ayn al-yaqin*); and third, that which comes from direct experience (*haqq al-yaqin*). This means that if a person does not truly understand what they believe to be the truth relative to their knowledge, then they have no certainty or true understanding. If a person's faith in God, the Qur'an as well as the other essential tenets of belief have not been induced or based on knowledge, if they have not considered, studied or related the events of the universe with the evidence provided, then this is not because of limited certainty; rather, such a person has no certainty at all. Certainty begins with knowledge; anything less is the lowest level of human understanding and life.

Knowledge is the first step to certainty. The book of the universe displays its wonders and miracles to the extent that scientists, artists and many other persons of knowledge have arrived at the conviction that such magnificence, orderliness and harmony in existence necessitates an All-Knowing and All-Wise Creator, and through such conviction have come to form the connection between the Qur'an and the universe. It is here when no doubt is left in one's mind about the All-Existent One that the first stage of certainty, that of knowledge, occurs.

The certainty of knowledge is the level at which one recognizes the manifestations of God, the Manifest One on all entities, when they have an understanding and full awareness that the universe with all its contents are all creations of God. This is the level at which a genuine and purposeful appreciation of all our surroundings awakens in one's consciousness and heart. The blooming of flowers, the singing of birds, the fruit-offering branches of trees opening to the skies and the sound of the gushing water of the river, those pure creations continue their search for their Creator like that of Majnun[8] for his Layla, thinking that every shadow, vision or sign he saw was what he was in search of.

---

[8]   In Sufi literature, the symbolic character Majnun stands for an initiate. He falls in desperate love with Layla. In the long run, the initiate's transitive love turns into divine love.

One achieves the certainty of faith by reaching a peak in faith at which one lives by the instructions of his Creator, when sincere comprehension that existence comes from God takes place. This is when those of faith understand the words of scholars who believed that: *"Everything comes from the Creator."* At this level of faith belief that animate and the inanimate comes to existence and continues its existence only through God's the command.

The truth of the matter is that all of these levels of certainty are interconnected; they support and compliment one another. In order not to be included in one of the categories that he feared most, it is important to attain at the least one of these degrees of belief.

If we were to draw a pattern and connect the major themes of this Hadith, then it can be ascertained that certainty of faith becomes almost impossible to attain if eating and drinking becomes the major goal in life. Certainty is granted for those who live in awe and sheer wonderment about the finest fruit of universe that is called life; it is for those who regulate their consumption patterns for the sake of living not just for pleasure.

To emphasize the magnitude of this subject the Prophet of God imparted that: *"The son of Adam fills no vessel that is worse than his stomach. It is sufficient for the son of Adam to eat a few mouthfuls to keep him alive. If he must do that (fill his stomach), then let him fill one third with food, one third with drink and one third with air."*

عَنْ عُثْمَانَ بْنِ عَفَّانِ رَضِيَ اللهُ عَنْهُ يَقُولُ قَالَ رَسُولُ اللهِ صَلَّى اللهُ عَلَيْهِ وَسَلَّمَ:

مَنْ قَالَ فِي أَوَّلِ يَوْمِهِ أَوْ فِي أَوَّلِ لَيْلَتِهِ بِسْمِ اللهِ الَّذِي لَا يَضُرُّ مَعَ اسْمِهِ شَيْءٌ

فِي الْأَرْضِ وَلَا فِي السَّمَاءِ وَهُوَ السَّمِيعُ الْعَلِيمُ

ثَلَاثَ مَرَّاتٍ لَمْ يَضُرَّهُ شَيْءٌ فِي ذَلِكَ الْيَوْمِ أَوْ فِي تِلْكَ اللَّيْلَةِ

⑧

A PRAYER OF PROTECTION FROM HARM

If any servant of God says at the beginning of the morning and/or in the evening: "In the name of God, by Whose name nothing in the earth or in the heaven can do any harm, He is All-Hearing, All-Knowing!" three times, nothing will harm him that day and night.

(Ibn Maja, Dua, 14; Ahmad ibn Hanbal, Musnad, 1:62)

There is a widespread belief that whoever supplicates this prayer would not suffer from paralysis. This is said to be because Aban Ibn Uthman who has reported this particular hadith was partially paralyzed. This may be the reason why the efficacy of this prayer has been connected with paralysis, but it is important to point out that this hadith carries a general meaning and is not focused on paralysis alone.

In this physical world, anyone can be inflicted with an illness or disability, be it via disease or due to paralysis. One could suffer from heart disease, or an infection, or clot in the veins could reach the brain, causing a stroke, paralyzing the whole body This is what is meant in the phrase *"in the earth"* refers to in the hadith; people who live in this world of temptation must take precautions and seek cure for any condition that might lead to more serious diseases or illnesses.

There may be certain people, who are endowed with clear insight and the ability to see beyond the veils of things, and they can observe that the effort made in the world of causes may be of no use; such people can say *"there is no need for a cure."* However, average people, as long as they live in the universe of means and causes, are compelled to and responsible for observing the laws of this world.

Another reason for illness is Divine will, referred to in the hadith as *"in the heaven"*; it is Divine will if a person is suddenly inflicted by paralysis, with no warning or for no apparent. Whatever the reason, in such situations a person must seek refuge with their Creator; the treatment, the power to cure, and the blessing of good health all belong to the Creator alone; if such a situation is looked at from the human senses, then seeking refuge in God is the only acceptable or logical step one can take. If there is no apparent remedy, then we have no option but to seek refuge with the Creator. As İbrahim Hakkı said:

> *When things come to a dead end,*
> *Providence will lend a hand,*
> *For every kind of wound to mend.*
> *Whatever it is that God ordains,*
> *It is sure to be goodness.*

We usually pray to God for mercy and for health; as in the prayer *"O God, I seek your forgiveness and protection."* We pray for forgiveness from all kinds of malice and spiritual diseases and for protection against all material diseases and illnesses. Although harm or disability is not mentioned in the prayer, we can see the relationship between health and sin in the words "protection" and "forgiveness." Let us expand on a few points.

> *"God has sent down the disease and the cure; for every disease there is a cure. Take medicine, but do not use anything that is forbidden (haram) as treatment"* (Abu Dawud, Tib, 11).

According to this hadith, there is a cure for every disease or illness, including paralysis. This cure may sometimes be obtained with a physical remedy or treatment, while in other cases it is possible to be cured without any apparent treatment, but rather with a direct supplication to God for the blessing of health.

For example, one of the recommendations of Prophet Muhammad, peace and blessings be upon him, regarding this subject was to place the hand on the area that is in pain and recite "*Bismillah*" three times, and then recite the prayer meaning "I seek refuge in God and His Power from the evil that afflicts me and that which I fear."[9]

If this is done with a sincere heart then complete faith in God has been demonstrated and there is a possibility that we may be granted health or the cure we have asked for. That is, the sincere prayer of a believer counts as purity of servitude and when it reaches the Gates of Divinity all causes may well be overcome and surmounted, thus making it possible that the ill person will be blessed with a special cure from God, or "the mystery of power from the light of unification."

When a person is afflicted with any kind of disease or illness they feel low-spirited and the cells in the body's are similarly affected. However, with deep sincere belief, and the mental resoluteness and positivity that "I *can* overcome this illness" with the help of God, it is possible to defeat an illness as serious as cancer. It is possible that the body can overcome an illness with spiritual power and, naturally, with the person's sincere belief in their Creator. When the cells are induced with such a great belief this is reflected in the body, a belief that can cause the cells to recuperate, this in turn enables the body to react in a positive way. The cells will thrive on the great spirit of the patient and renew themselves, gaining strength, fighting against disease and even curing the most fatal illnesses.

In one of the weaker hadith[10] the Prophet stated: "*Each person is protected by more than three hundred angels.*" These angels are on guard, possibly conditional on fulfilling the requirements of the physical world and not ignoring medical treatment—and maybe some of them guard us even without such a condition. This is the reason why a believer should always mention the angels in their prayers as well. The supplication in the hadith

---

9   *A'udhu bi'izzatillahi wa qudratihi min sharri ma ajidu wa 'uhadhiru*

10   Hadith have been categorized according to the strength of their authentication. Weaker hadith refers to those reports that may have some level of uncertainty in the chain of narrators as the hadith was relayed.

can also be seen to be a call to the angels to protect one against harm and evil. It is very important that all Muslims recite this prayer three times every morning and every night.

The reporter of this hadith, Aban Ibn Uthman, suffered from partial paralysis. He noticed that one of the Companions was looking at him and it appeared as if he wanted to ask Aban about his condition. He explained that the hadith was correct as he had reported, but that he forgot to recite that prayer on the day he was paralyzed (Ibn Maja, Dua, 14).

A summation of the supplication is: *"God is all hearing and all knowing"*— The first word of this, all knowing or omniscience is *'Alim.'* This is one of the most comprehensive attributes of Almighty God, which encompasses everything. God has pervasive knowledge of all that exists and does not exist; only such a Being of such great power and knowledge could have planned what we call fate or destiny. This power ranges from the planning of the great values of the macrocosm, which affects the universe as a whole, to minute details in matters at the microcosm level, like the blockage of a human vein for example.

The next word is *"Sami,"* which means "All Hearing." The greatest being who hears everything will also hear this prayer; thus, with the statements *"No harm will come to those who recite this prayer"* and "The person reciting this prayer is guaranteed of the blessings reported in the hadith" we can understand that "All Knowing" and "All Hearing" means that our prayers are known and heard by He who knows and hears all.

As a result, whether or not we understand how, this prayer taught to us by one of the greatest of Prophets still is and will continue to be valid. May God place us among those servants of His who are blessed with belief in this and in all the other tenets of truth within the depths of their souls. Amin!

عَنْ أَبِي هُرَيْرَةَ عَنِ النَّبِيِّ صَلَّى اللهُ عَلَيْهِ وَسَلَّمَ قَالَ:
تَعَلَّمُوا مِنْ أَنْسَابِكُمْ مَا تَصِلُونَ بِهِ أَرْحَامَكُمْ فَإِنَّ صِلَةَ الرَّحِمِ
مَحَبَّةٌ فِي الْأَهْلِ مَثْرَاةٌ فِي الْمَالِ مَنْسَأَةٌ فِي الْأَثَرِ

⑨

THE VALUE OF FAMILY TIES

"Know your relatives to maintain family bonds with (sila al-rahm[11]). Surely, maintaining family bonds results in love between relatives, increase in wealth and lengthening in one's life."

(Tirmidhi, Birr, 49; Ahmad ibn Hanbal, Musnad, 2:374)

The relationship between Prophet Adam and Prophet David must be one of the greatest examples of the extension of one's lifespan. Prophet Adam bequeathed forty years of his own life to Prophet David, who thought his own lifetime was too short to achieve what he needed to; thus Prophet David's time on this earth was extended by forty years, increasing his lifespan to eighty years. Although this event is

---

[11] Visiting one's relatives, asking after them, helping and supporting them, and treating them kindly and generously.

not mentioned in the Qur'an, it is related by the most important hadiths sources like Bukhari and Muslim.

From the early periods, the subject of transfer of a person's lifetime to another as a consequence of relevant prayers was a recognized phenomenon between saintly people; however, such a thing can only be realized given that there is conformity between the spiritual worlds of the people in question, that the prayer is perfectly sincere, for God answers the supplication in the same way it was asked for. Perhaps, a similar case of sincere devotion can be realized when the rights of relatives are observed and in this way the Permanent Existent One, God Almighty may extend the lifetime of that person.

Another reason why the Giver of Life, extends one's life could be the possibility of rendering the deeds of that person more fruitful as if he or she lived a longer life; if the reward in the Hereafter depends on the deeds and good actions one has performed in this physical world then the longer the term, the greater its harvest in the permanent realm. For instance the *Night of Power* is recognized by all Muslims to be greater in reward than a thousand months of worship; if a believer manages to tap into the Divine Mercy during this night they will be rewarded as if they have lived on the earth for more than eighty years. This could be God's way of increasing good deeds, acts of charity and the lives of sincere believers.

Another possibility why family relations are considered to prolong one's life is perhaps proportional to the importance given to family ties. This undoubtedly is a highly esteemed principle in Islam but in modern times, unfortunately has become widely neglected.

It is very important to regularly visit family members in turn, beginning with close family, mothers and fathers, sisters and brothers, grandparents and then aunts and uncles. In the recent times respect for the nearest of kin, like one's own mother or father has unfortunately dropped to regrettable lows. When after receiving the first revelations of the Qur'an the Prophet told his wife Khadija: *"I fear for myself,"* [12] the intimate companion and beloved wife of the Prophet answered, saying: *"Do not fear; by God, He*

---

[12] The noble Prophet uttered these words just after he had encountered Archangel Gabriel at Mount Hira, for the first time. Trying to make sense of the intense and extraordinary experience, the Prophet rushed to his home and related the story to his beloved Khadijah.

will never humiliate you. You maintain the family bonds, you bear people's burdens, and you help the destitute." It is quite clear by her statement and also by a similar statement made by her cousin Waraqa ibn Nawfal that during that period family relationships were of significant importance.

When the noble Prophet was being oppressed by the unbelievers, Abu Bakr said: "*O Messenger of God! One like you, who helps the poor and maintains family bonds, does not deserve this!*" Again when he was seeking protection from the Quraysh for his fellow Companions, Prophet Muhammad, peace and blessings be upon him, mentioned family bonds in his appeal.

All these different scenarios and contexts are revealing of the strong custom of family ties. Throughout history, the likes of similar reports about kinship demonstrate the eminent role that families played across many different civilizations. In earlier times sons and daughters would live along with their parents and children in the same home; this practice of extended family settings are still the norm in some parts of the world. Since family is the basic unit of society, the greater the bond and affection between them, the stronger and healthier the society is.

عَنِ الْمُغِيرَةِ بْنِ شُعْبَةَ قَالَ قَالَ النَّبِيُّ صَلَّى اللهُ عَلَيْهِ وَسَلَّمَ:
إِنَّ اللَّهَ حَرَّمَ عَلَيْكُمْ عُقُوقَ الْأُمَّهَاتِ وَوَأْدَ الْبَنَاتِ وَمَنَعَ وَهَاتِ
وَكَرِهَ لَكُمْ قِيلَ وَقَالَ وَكَثْرَةَ السُّؤَالِ وَإِضَاعَةَ الْمَالِ

⑩

THE THREE THINGS FORBIDDEN (*HARAM*) AND THE THREE THINGS DISAPPROVED OF (*MAKRUH*)

"God has forbidden you from disobeying your mothers, from burying new born daughters alive, from not honoring the rights and debts that have been incurred, and receiving whatever you do not have a right to. He dislikes tittle-tattle, questioning excessively, and dissipating wealth."

(Bukhari, Istiqrad, 19; Muslim, Aqdiya, 12)

In this hadith the words used for disobedience against mothers, *uquq al-ummahat*, carries quite a harsh tone with it, so that the act of one who opposes or disobeys their mother is highlighted, the use of literary infuriated tone against those who actually destroy the bond of the

32

mother-child relationship and as a result abandon their mother completely is quite dissuading. Of course, disobedience towards one's father is also forbidden, but one of the reasons why only mothers are mentioned here is because their kindhearted nature can be taken advantage of. Although the father has the same rights as the mother in regard to respect and even though opposing one's father is a form of rebellion and defiance, nevertheless it can in no way be compared to the weight of disobeying one's mother.

The outrageous practice of burying baby girls alive during the Time of Ignorance is referred in this hadith as *"wa'd al-banat."* Many baby girls born into various communities in different regions were buried alive by their fathers during the pre-Islamic period. This cruel and contemptible custom was practiced by some out of obvious ignorance, for others perhaps because of poverty, while for the others it was a way to keep their wealth from being passed onto strangers when their daughters were married off to those families. Irrespective of the reason or in this case the lack thereof, this barbarity had to be stopped. As a result many commands and orders were revealed in both the Qur'an and the hadiths.

The word *"mana'a"* (as forbidden) refers to the dishonoring of rights and debts incurred, whereas demanding and grabbing what is not one's is expressed with the word *"haati."* Both deeds are clearly forbidden or *haram* and are mentioned in the same sentence as the disobedience shown towards one's parents and the burial of baby daughter alive.

We come to the conclusion that the first word indicates the responsibility towards the poor; this could entail alms, charity or any other kind of donation, while the second word is directed towards beggars and those who ask for charity. If we go one step further and elaborate on this explanation, the first word actually means denying the rights of others or keeping what does not belong to us; this could mean anything from eliminating the practices of unpaid cheques or bills to fraudulent bankruptcy or illegal earnings of any kind.

The second word can be interpreted to mean begging, exploiting religious or national feelings, or anything in connection with this, legal or illegal; if we take this last connotation even further, it is possible that it refers to extortionists who openly benefit from the innocence of others, who use their mob connections to scrounge, steal or extort from innocent people.

Three other topics also mentioned in the hadith are, even if they are not as grave as the previous one, tittle-tattle, asking unnecessary questions, and making a habit of begging, waste and extravagance.

Qiyla wa qaala means tittle-tattle, or unnecessary chitchat. Without going into too many details, let us look at the actual meaning. The expression means unnecessary speech that has no significance or beneficial aspect in this world or the Hereafter. We can call this idle chat, gossip or conversation about a subject that has no real importance or significance; according to the social standing of those who gossip and the extent of the spread of gossip, this can also include declarations or reports in the media (newspapers, magazines, radio and television. This has become a social disease that creates groups and communities of idle, heedless individuals who have no true aim in life. Gossip is strongly dissuaded in Islam and it is for this reason that the Prophet included empty talk when discussing subjects that are disapproved of in Islam:

> *"Let he who believes in God and the Last Day not inconvenience his neighbor; let he who believes in God and the Last Day be generous to his guests; let he who believes in God and the Last Day either speak good or keep silent...!"*

Asking unnecessary questions, speaking to no real purpose or just talking for the sake of conversation are unacceptable and can be harmful. Excessive or unnecessary speech is disapproved of both in the Qur'an and the hadith; however, with every possible opportunity humans are encouraged to learn about beneficial topics.

The subject of asking questions or begging falls into the category of acceptable or disapproved actions, ranking between necessary to forbidden, depending on whether they source from a real obligation or need. Therefore, it is more appropriate to consider and interpret these two seemingly different matters together in terms of the "common aspect" they have.

"Dissipating wealth or belongings" is a problem globally suffered today. The excessive use of wealth with no material or spiritual advantages or benefits in this world or the Hereafter is a disease of both individuals and society. Even though dissipating personal wealth may at first seem to harm only the individual, on a long-term basis it indirectly affects the national assets, which in turn causes damage to the economy of the nation as a whole.

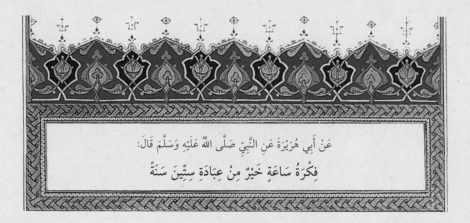

عَنْ أَبِي هُرَيْرَةَ عَنِ النَّبِيِّ صَلَّى اللهُ عَلَيْهِ وَسَلَّمَ قَالَ:
فِكْرَةُ سَاعَةٍ خَيْرٌ مِنْ عِبَادَةِ سِتِّينَ سَنَةً

REFLECTION AND WORSHIP

*"Reflection (tafakkur) for one hour is better than sixty years
of (supererogatory) worship."*

(Kanz al-Ummal, 3:106)

I
n this hadith it is stated that one hour of reflection is equal to sixty years
of supererogatory worship, while in another report the latter time period is given as one year; however, the latter hadith is said to be a weaker
one. There are many verses in the Qur'an that confirm this matter:

> Surely in the creation of the heavens and the earth and the alternation of
> night and day (with their periods shortening and lengthening), there are signs
> (manifesting the truth) for the people of discernment. (Al-Imran 3:190)

There is a lesson and sign for those who reflect on the wonders of the
universe; the dazzling display of the continual rotation and movement of
the sun and moon with immaculate precision, as well as their rising and
setting in incredible harmony. Regarding the question of reflection, the
holy Prophet said: *"Shame on he who recites this verse and gives it no thought."*
Umm Salama reported that the Prophet wept when this verse was revealed
and he also wept whenever he recited it. This and many other verses are
windows and gates that open the doors of thought and lead to the path

of reflection; they are very important for displaying the dimensions of the world of thought in Islam.

First, we must understand the true meaning of reflection; it has to be based on certain initial knowledge. In other words, thinking without a foundation does not lead us to true reflection. Over a matter of time confined thought will lead to boredom and then it will stagnate. A human must first know and understand the subject of thought and then form the basis of this knowledge into a supply of practical information in the mind; in other words, a person must have knowledge of the past and of their environs so that they can think systematically.

The orbit of the moon and stars astonishes one and these movements have a profound influence on humanity. When one thinks over the wonder works that is extensively displayed across the universe, if one is able to recognize and understand even a little of what is going on around one then this is reflection.[13] But, if you look into the skies only with romantic inspiration from poetry, you will only be a dreamer telling his inspirations. True reflection requires a certain background of knowledge, discernment of present realities, making new derivations in conformity with the essence knowledge, and applying oneself in quest of continuum for the truth.

One who systematizes one's thoughts with such a coherent technique will reach deeper stages of thought which will open and the lead the way for advanced thoughts in other topics, and this in turn will lead to unprecedented results and a deeper aspect of reflection. Thus, one-dimensional forms of thought will turn into two and three-dimensional reflection; in time, as these perceptions or dimensions increase, the reflecting person can attain the level of spiritual perfection, or *insan al-kamil*.[14]

The first principle of thought is knowing, reading and familiarizing oneself with the Book of the Universe, opening the soul to the inspirations from the Creator, opening the mind to the principles of the laws of creation, and viewing the existence from the perspective of its sacred interpretation, the Qur'an. Although the concepts, their goals and intentions are undetermined, an ignorant perception of objects or events can not be considered to be reflection; with such a backdrop, there can be no possi-

---

[13]   See www.fountainmagazine.com for exemplifications of this perspective. (Ed.)
[14]   See Key Concepts in the Practice of Sufism vol II., Tughra Books.

bility of any real progress in thought and the rewards will always remain open to question.

The reason why an hour of reflection equals to years of worship is that human beings have been endowed the capacity to reach at the heart of faith potentially within an hour's intense and qualitative thought, their souls will glow from the light of accomplishment and their hearts will be overwhelmed by Divine affection. They then can reap the pure pleasures of spirituality, achieving in such a short time what those deprived of thought are only able to achieve in a thousand months.

If however a person with no real understanding or sense of reflection worships continuously for a thousand years this in no way equals to an hour of reflection; such a person will exhibit no sign of true progress unless they attain the grace and favor of their Creator directly. This however does not mean that this worship or these actions were performed in vain; for no prayer, prostration or any form of worship for the sake of The Worshipped One is done in vain. The depth and quality though varies in proportion to the quality of thought and therefore the level of reflection that has been tapped into.

عَنْ عَلِيٍّ رَضِيَ اللَّهُ عَنْهُ قَالَ قَالَ رَسُولُ اللَّهِ صَلَّى اللَّهُ عَلَيْهِ وَسَلَّمَ:

أَدَّبَنِي رَبِّي فَأَحْسَنَ تَأْدِيبِي

(12)

GOOD MANNERS

"God gave me good manners (adab), and He rendered my manners in the best way."

(Kanz al-Ummal, 7:214)

*A*dab is an Arabic word for literature, which has a wider frame of connotation associated with good manners, gentleness, elegance, refinement, and perfection. It has often been interpreted in relation to a person's lifestyle, conduct, and integrity and as a means to the flourishing of that person in spirituality and purification of the heart. The Messenger of God is the paragon of *adab*. No matter which meaning of the word *adab* is considered as far as this hadith is concerned, good manners or power of expression, the Messenger of God is always the epitome of both.

One day Abu Bakr asked the Prophet: *"O Messenger of God! Who gave you such good manners?"* The Prophet replied: *"God gave me adab (good manners) and He rendered my manners in the best way."*

Aisha, the daughter of Abu Bakr and the wife of the Prophet, was asked about the morals of the Prophet. She replied: *"Don't you ever read the Qur'an?"* Her audience answered to the affirmative. She then continued: *"His morals were the Qur'an."*

The Prophet was granted such great manners by the Creator that he reached the peak of morality; those who seek the real meaning of manners should examine the courteous Prophet's actions and behavior and transfer this into their own way of living.

God created His Messenger with the greatest manners and behavior, as a model to all mankind; on the contrary, it is difficult to imagine the great burden that the noble Prophet shouldered with such a mission. He carried the responsibility of all his followers. If Prophet Muhammad, peace and blessings be upon him, had not been endowed with such exalted mannerism it is likely that he would have made errors in his behavior like any ordinary person; however, unlike the rest of us, his mistakes would have been reflected and amplified by his followers. Prophet Muhammad was not answerable for himself alone; rather, he shouldered the responsibility for his entire community. This is why God created His Messenger with outstanding morals and behavior and sent Him as a beautiful example for mankind.

Prophet Muhammad was known for his good deeds and actions; sometime prior to his Prophethood, restoration work was being carried out in Ka'ba. The Messenger helped the workers to repair and rebuild the holy house. His uncle Abbas threw his gown over his shoulder to prevent any stones from injuring him. He saw that the Prophet's shoulder was grazed and sore from the heavy stones, so his uncle advised him to do the same; however doing so would have exposed the upper part of his thigh (which was later forbidden by Islam). Suddenly an angel appeared before him and the Prophet fainted, falling to the ground. He never again contemplated on such a thought, for he was under the protection of the Creator, even well before his Prophethood.

The Prophet once said: *"I had the intention of taking part in a wedding ceremony when I was young, and on both occasions I was overpowered by sleep; when I woke up the wedding had long finished."*

These are all events that happened before he was blessed with the Prophethood.

Throughout his lifetime God never gave his Messenger any reason or the opportunity to commit any inappropriate action in any way; this is an exceptional condition that was granted to the Prophet alone.

It is not surprising that this was the case, for when he was a young child his chest was opened by the angels and any tendency or trace of evil was removed. The target of the Devil's arrow, the black spot that is found in every human heart, was removed from the Prophet's heart when he was very young. The Devil instigates within us apprehension and suspicion, he runs through our veins, impelling us to evil; but he was unable to even approach God's Messenger, for he was an exceptional person.

The Almighty never gave his Messenger the chance to do evil or to sin, either prior to or during his Prophethood; he lived a life of purity from the day he was born until he departed from the universe and he was the embodiment of good manners.

The good manners and behavior of Prophet Muhammad, peace be upon him, remained with him throughout his entire life; his every move or action reflected his virtuous manners. Although it was a rare occasion, the Prophet became upset or frustrated upon certain cases, but this too was due to his good manners as well. There was always a valid reason for his anger, and it was in response to injustice.

A Bedouin came to the Prophet while he was with the Companions and harshly pulling at the Prophet's collar, demanded justice; the Bedouin pulled the Prophet's collar so hard that a mark remained on his neck. This greatly upset the Companions, but the Prophet just smiled and told him in a calm voice, *"Give this man what he asks for."* This event is one of the hundreds of examples that indicates the depth and breadth of Prophet Muhammad's great tolerance.

There are many situations in which even the most sedate person justly becomes annoyed or frustrated, but even under these conditions the morals of the Prophet shone through like the gleaming sun. The following is just one of the most dramatic examples:

The Prophet had dream shortly before setting out for the Battle of Uhud; this dream led the Prophet to believe that remaining in Medina and forming a defensive battle would be more appropriate, and he approached the Companions saying, *"We should remain in Medina."* However, the Companions were so excited and keen to fight for the sake of Islam that such excitement clouded their judgment.

So they set off for Uhud, with the Prophet personally taking command and organizing the army in the best possible way; the enemy began to flee after the first attack, but the archers had not grasped the fine point of obeying the Prophet's command accurately and abandoned their posts.

As a result, sixty-nine Muslims was martyred, among them the Prophet's uncle Hamza; every man on the battlefield was injured and some of them carried the pain of these wounds for the rest of their lives. But even more importantly, the greatest injury for the Muslims was that the honor of Islam had been damaged.

Such behavior by an army would have angered any other leader and under normal circumstances the Prophet could have treated those around him harshly; but God the Omniscient prevented the Prophet from acting harshly, protecting and guiding him. God revealed:

> *It was by a mercy from God that (at the time of the setback), you (O Messenger) were lenient with them (your Companions). Had you been harsh and hard-hearted, they would surely have scattered away from about you. Then pardon them, pray for their forgiveness, and take counsel with them in the affairs (of public concern); and when you are resolved (on a course of action), put your trust in God. Surely God loves those who put their trust (in Him).*
> (Al- Imran 3:159)

The Prophet was a person who commanded great respect; indeed, the Merciful One addressed His Messenger in the same way. For instance, instead of saying *"Do not be harsh hearted,"* the Creator addressed the Prophet, revealing: *"Had you been harsh and hard-hearted,"* that is, *"you are not harsh."*

عَنْ أَبِي أُمَامَةَ الْبَاهِلِيِّ قَالَ قَالَ رَسُولُ اللهِ صَلَّى اللهُ عَلَيْهِ وَسَلَّمَ:
فَضْلُ الْعَالِمِ عَلَى الْعَابِدِ كَفَضْلِي عَلَى أَدْنَاكُمْ

KNOWLEDGE AND WORSHIP

*"The superiority of a scholar to an ordinary worshipper is the same
as my superiority to a man of the lowest level among you."*

(Tirmidhi, Ilm, 19)

The hadith above is how the Prophet explained the virtues of being a scholar. There is always the chance that a worshipping believer without much knowledge could make a mistake and stray from the true path; there is even the possibility of deviation. The level of deviation depends on a person's relationship with the Creator. There are some people who believe that if the thought of God leaves their minds for a single moment this is a serious sign of deviation. Those who carry on the legacy of Prophet Muhammad, the learned and wise men of the world are in a constant state of self-supervision and they examine their own actions and thoughts continuously. They are always aware and alert of the potential dangers they may face. A scholar who performs their religious duties and considers every matter in a conscious manner is as elevated over those who worship with no knowledge or consciousness as the Prophet is over his Companions.

Another explanation of this hadith is that a person who reaches perfection of faith will never miss an opportunity to gain more knowledge, and thus they make every effort to absorb every ray of light they possibly can in their heart; this in turn is transmitted to the soul as a manifestation of unity with the Creator. It develops and flourishes into a sense of compassion that inflames one's feelings towards the Creator.

At the same time, this is an expression of a person's esteem for God, a means of re-instilling the soul with spiritual emotions and the manifestations of the truth; the gleams of light that are absorbed into the soul are conveyed onto others. There is no limit to the knowledge or satisfaction of worship for a person of such wisdom.

It is the duty of every human being to practice and convey that of which they have knowledge; on the contrary, those who do not act accordingly are warned about in the following verse of the Qur'an: *Yet a party among them conceal the truth, and they do it knowingly* (Baqara 2:146). Some people have knowledge but they neither practice it nor convey it to others, keeping what they know in their souls without giving others the opportunity to benefit from their knowledge. These pitiful, helpless people refrain from spreading these rays of light into the souls of others. Although they have the capability and means of radiating the light of prosperity, the spiritual emotions that emanate from their souls are confined to their knowledge within a prison of darkness.

It is stated in another hadith about the same subject that whoever acquires knowledge and keeps it concealed, God will bridle him with a bridle of fire on the Day of Resurrection. The meaning of these words is quite clear; whoever learns something beneficial but confines it to their soul, whoever does not portray this knowledge into their words or actions as an example for others will be punished in the Hereafter.

This hadith is a rebuke and a condemnation; a bridle is an object placed in the mouths of animals. Such people give no significance to the outstanding virtues of thought and knowledge and have no gratitude for the merits and virtues that have been bestowed upon them, and as such they are deprived of the various mysteries of the beauty of faith and the emotions of belief that transform humankind into a being that is separate from all other creatures.

Knowledge and conveyance of knowledge are two different aspects of the same phenomenon, whereas worship is necessary from the aspect of belief; when the three are integrated they become an inseparable, indistinguishable expression of religion. Practicing what we know is an expression of our respect towards knowledge. A person who acknowledges the Creator but has no inclination to worship or abide by God's commands not only displays disrespect, but is also completely ignorant and heedless.

Particularly negligence of duties of faith by those who are supposed to represent their religion leave a far worse impression on the image of Islam then perhaps other outer factors. The expressions and comments of people in the West after having seen the Muslims who do not practice their religion are living proof of this; these comments will be enough of a testimony in the Hereafter.

To explain briefly, Islam is a Divine system which integrates faith and action. It is belief combined with the individual's duty of worship and certain daily practices. Giving explanation about the experiences and actions of others is a positive action, because such narratives can act as an example of inspiration for others to follow. However, living the practices and duties of faith is the best and most effective way to portray these experiences to others. As a matter of fact, narrating these experiences without personally living them will only have a negative effect on the impression that others may have of Muslims. Islam is not merely about explaining or listening to stories of the wise and holy men of religion; it is living and putting such wisdom into practice in our daily lives. Islam is an integration of faith and action and whoever speaks about the duties of faith and Islam yet finds that they cannot do the same in their own lives, actually speaks in vain, for their words will in essence bear no impact whatsoever.

عَنْ جَابِرِ بْنِ عَبْدِ اللهِ قَالَ قَالَ رَسُولُ اللهِ صَلَّى اللهُ عَلَيْهِ وَسَلَّمَ:
مَثَلِي وَمَثَلُكُمْ كَمَثَلِ رَجُلٍ أَوْقَدَ نَارًا فَجَعَلَ الْجَنَادِبُ وَالْفَرَاشُ يَقَعْنَ فِيهَا
وَهُوَ يَذُبُّهُنَّ عَنْهَا وَأَنَا آخِذٌ بِحُجَزِكُمْ عَنِ النَّارِ وَأَنْتُمْ تَفَلَّتُونَ مِنْ يَدِي

(14)

COMPASSION: THE PATH TO GUIDANCE
AND COMMUNICATION

"You and I are like the person who lights a fire and the insects and moths begin to fall into it and he makes an effort to remove them. I am holding you back from the fire, but you are slipping from my hands."

(Bukhari, Riqaq, 26; Muslim, Fadail, 17–19)

I t is impossible to solve any personal or social problem without being able to forgive people for their mistakes or faults, and showing
them the truth with compassion. This is why the Prophet made himself an example regarding the mistakes of his followers. These examples

of the Prophet Muhammad, peace and blessings be upon him, opened a great path towards guidance in Islam. This example implies that if this is the path chosen it could be the means of reaching many people. Views that are contrary to this, i.e. not approaching people with compassion, will make the matter shallow, will degenerate it, and—at the worst—it will lead some people totally astray.

But if you can approach people of today with a heart of compassion you will be able to listen to their problems with a soul that has a depth of emotion. It is not possible for a person who lives a life surrounded by sin or who is struggling in the waves of misery, to be happy; nobody wants to remain thus of their own free will, except for those whose conscience has fallen into darkness or whose soul is in a state of total decay. There are reasons for such conditions; a person may have fallen into this situation due to a simple error and could be searching for a way to escape. Your compassion and words of comfort might just be their path to this escape.

A person who is approached with compassion, care, and moderation will have a gentler and calmer response, even if they disagree with what is being said. It is a fact that there have been many people, hundreds and maybe thousands, whose souls have opened up when it was most unexpected. If you reach out and help others, due to your sense of compassion and understanding, such people can reach the light of faith. They will be eternally grateful in their souls for your help, and of course you will also be rewarded in the Hereafter with a share of every good deed that they may perform.

We can elaborate on this topic with a few examples. Imagine that a person you dislike has been caught in a fire with his wife and children, or perhaps the survivors of a sinking ship are struggling to swim to safety, hoping to be saved by you, a complete stranger. Without giving a second thought, you would do what any other person, with any sense of humanity, would do; you would make every effort possible to save them, even if others were trying to prevent you. This is what your conscience orders you to do and the voice of the conscience is more effective than any other thing that anyone else may say.

In these times when humanity is being led into material and spiritual disasters that impact our lives, we must examine the situation and conditions from every angle and then give advice or intervene accordingly; it would not be right for a wise person, one who represents Islam, to participate in violence, abuse or force. They must distance themselves from lies and political interests at all times. Believers only exist to help out to others with love, affection, and compassion for the sake of God; this is what is needed and expected by those who are awaiting guidance. Prophet Muhammad, peace and blessings be upon him, is the greatest guide and the best example for us to follow; just imagine what he put up with for the sake of saving others' faith. These even included people who would abuse and throw stones or foul objects at him, attempting to strangle him while he was praying.

He was stoned by the Taif community; covered in blood, he sought refuge under a tree in an orchard. The angel of the mountains appeared and told the Prophet that they were ready to crush the mountain over this disobedient nation if he wished; but the Prophet wished no harm upon these people and with his great compassion, he said that he hoped that God would send persons from among their nation who would worship Him.

Another clear demonstration of the Prophet's sincere compassion was when his tooth was broken and a part from his metal helmet lodged into his cheek during a battle; with blood pouring down his face the Prophet held his hands and pleaded with the Creator: *"O my Lord, guide this nation for they know not,"* thus preventing any disaster from befalling them.

There is nothing to gain from feelings of resentment or harsh actions. Our duty is to serve humanity towards universal human values; force is not a method to be undertaken unnecessarily, nor should it ever be used when guiding others.

عَنْ عَبْدِ اللهِ بْنِ مَسْعُودٍ رَضِيَ اللهُ عَنْهُ قَالَ قَالَ رَسُولُ اللهِ صَلَّى اللهُ عَلَيْهِ وَسَلَّمَ:

عَلَيْكُمْ بِالصِّدْقِ فَإِنَّ الصِّدْقَ يَهْدِي إِلَى الْبِرِّ وَإِنَّ الْبِرَّ يَهْدِي إِلَى الْجَنَّةِ وَمَا

يَزَالُ الرَّجُلُ يَصْدُقُ وَيَتَحَرَّى الصِّدْقَ حَتَّى يُكْتَبَ عِنْدَ اللهِ صِدِّيقًا وَإِيَّاكُمْ

وَالْكَذِبَ فَإِنَّ الْكَذِبَ يَهْدِي إِلَى الْفُجُورِ وَإِنَّ الْفُجُورَ يَهْدِي إِلَى النَّارِ وَمَا

يَزَالُ الرَّجُلُ يَكْذِبُ وَيَتَحَرَّى الْكَذِبَ حَتَّى يُكْتَبَ عِنْدَ اللهِ كَذَّابًا

⑮

THE OUTCOME OF HONESTY AND DECEIT

"Live honestly. Honesty leads to goodness and goodness leads to Paradise. Once a man has given himself over to honesty and heads in that direction, he will always speak the truth, always search for what is right. Thus, he will be recorded as "Siddiq" (Truthful) with God. Avoid lying. Lying leads to immorality and immorality leads to Hell. Once a man has given himself to lies will always lie. Thus he will be recorded as "Kazzab" (one who lies very much) with God."

(Bukhari, Adab, 69; Abu Dawud, Adab, 80)

Honesty is one of the characteristics that all the Prophets had, whereas lying or deceit is the sign of hypocrites and disbelievers. Honesty is an important part of our lives, affecting our past, present and future; deceit is a shadow of darkness that pursues us throughout our lives. Nobody has ever found happiness with deceit or lies and people on the path of truth and honesty will never be deprived in this world or in the Hereafter.

Deceit is the most evident characteristic of unbelief; it is the means of opposing that which God perceives and knows. Lying has destroyed the morals and principles of modern society; it is a social disease that has turned the world into a nation of deceitful beings. There is no salvation for those nations who open their doors to deceit, allowing it to flow freely into every aspect of their lives and their homes, businesses, their political dealings, or military posts. Nor will there be any salvation for them. This is the most significant aspect of the Islamic mission, the most evident awareness of faith, the foundation of the principles of Prophet Muhammad. This is the greatest feature of all the teachings of the Prophets and scholars; honesty is the only means to spiritual and material progress in the universe.

On one hand, we have the honored servant of God, Prophet Muhammad who is the Pride of Humanity; while on the other hand, we have the display of unbelief and corruption of the soul, an obvious trait of the devil.

The example of the first word in the hadith, *birr* (goodness), refers to purity of thought and action in human life; it is an expression of faith of such vast scope that it covers many aspects of life and favorable actions, including honest thought, honest speech, honest intentions, honest actions, and above all an honest way of living. However, the word *fujur* (immorality) is the complete opposite; it is the result of evil, it is the basis of deviant thought, speech, and evil actions, and it is an attribute of Hell.

In the hadith, a *siddiq* and a *kazzab* are mentioned side by side. The first has integrity, which indicates a person who has made honesty and truthfulness his way of life, the second example is one who has become a habitual liar. Both words are inflected to express the top level of the relevant adjective; accordingly a person who takes pride in their honesty, speaking and acting in a truthful manner, is sure to reach the affection of God at sometime during their life, while the person who takes pride in lying and who is dishonest in their everyday actions will become the epitome of dishonesty.

The final destination of these paths, although some are long and others short, although some gleam with light and security while others are misty and dangerous, is either Paradise or Hell. The path that leads to Paradise consists of various stages of blessings and encouragement, while the one that ends up in eternal disappointment consists of nothing but great disadvantages and obstructions.

The matter that we have tried to bring to everybody's attention here is what are the consequences of honesty in this world and in the Hereafter and the damage that dishonesty can do to both individuals and to society; if we have been able to convey this in such a brief explanation, this is due to the great words contained in the hadith of the Prophet.

50

عَنْ عَبْدِ اللهِ بْنِ مَسْعُودٍ رَضِيَ اللهُ عَنْهُ عَنِ النَّبِيِّ صَلَّى اللهُ عَلَيْهِ وَسَلَّمَ أَنَّهُ قَالَ:

الْمَرْءُ مَعَ مَنْ أَحَبَّ

(16)

ETERNAL COMPANY WITH THOSE WHOM YOU LOVE

"A person will be with those he loves"

(Bukhari, Adab, 96; Muslim, Birr, 165)

This hadith can be like a sip of water from the rivers of Paradise or the elixir of life for the many sad and brokenhearted people who have been unable to follow their guide on the path to truth and wisdom with due exertion or accuracy; with these words Prophet Muhammad, peace and blessings be upon him, tells us that a person will be with those they love, be they a good or bad person, in this world and in the Hereafter. Therefore, a person should have love and affection for those they long to be with, that is, the Prophets, the Companions or the martyrs, so they can be with them.

In other words, those who love and respect the Prophets, Companions and martyrs in this world of mortality will be with them in the Hereafter.

51

This also holds true for those who represent evil or bad actions; they will be with those they love and admire. This hadith, consisting of just one sentence, is not only expressed in a beautifully succinct manner; but it goes to show to those whose minds are open to revelation and inspiration, that such words surely emanated from a being who possessed the profound ability to utter an expression as such.

Nuayman was sometimes punished for drinking alcohol; even though what Nuayman had done was a sin, when one of the Companions cursed him, the Prophet frowned and said: *"Do not be an aid of the devil against your brother. I swear that he loves God and his Messenger"* (Bukhari, Hudud, 4, 5). It was not appropriate for anyone to curse Nuayman, because whatever other sins he may have committed, he loved God and his Messenger. Love for the Prophet and his Companions are sufficient to allow those who perform their religious duties and avoid major sins to be with Prophet Muhammad.

The Prophet left for a campaign but the Companion Sawban was unable to accompany him. On the Prophet's return everyone went to visit him, including Sawban. The latter looked very pale and had lost a great deal of weight; in fact, he was so thin his bones were showing. The Prophet of Compassion inquired: *"Sawban, what is wrong with you?"* Sawban replied: *"O Messenger of God! I am in this state because I have constantly thought about being apart from you; how will I be able to endure the eternal separation after death? You will ascend among the Prophets, so, even were I to reach Paradise, I would not be with you eternally."*

The Messenger of God gave him a timeless answer to cure his suffering: *"A person will be with those he loves."*

Loving someone means accepting their way of life and their actions as an example to follow in our own lives. The Companions were more aware of this than anyone else. Umar ibn al-Khattab spent his life hoping to become a member of the Prophet's family; at one time he thought of establishing a connection between himself and the Prophet by marrying the Prophet's daughter Fatima, who later married Ali. His main goal in life was to have some kind of familial connection with the Messenger of God. Umar could quite easily have married the Byzantine emperor's daughter, but his intention was to establish a tie with the Prophet and have a close relationship with the man he admired and loved more than anything in his life. This would have been a relationship from which he would benefit eternally.

Umar and the Prophet were close from the early days and there was a very strong spiritual tie between them; on many occasions the Prophet would hold Umar's hand, saying *"Our bond will continue in this world and in the Hereafter."* Umar, longing to strengthen the worldly tie between himself and God's Messenger, decided to give his daughter to the Prophet in marriage and Umar married Ali's daughter, the Prophet's granddaughter, Umm Kulthum. As one can imagine, this double connection pleased Umar very much. Thus we can see how one of the Companions made every effort to establish a closer relation with the Prophet, the person he loved more than anything in this world.

Another example of Umar's devotion to the Prophet is that one day Hafsa, Umar's daughter and the wife of Prophet Muhammad, went to her father and said, *"O father, you are continuously meeting the officials and the envoys of other states; don't you think it would be better if you had some new clothes to wear?"* Umar was shocked to hear these words, especially from his own daughter. Mentioning the Prophet and Abu Bakr, Umar replied, *"How can I be separated from those two people? I must live like them in this world so I will be with them in the Hereafter."*

The Prophet and his Companions lived in a constant state of greater *jihad* or struggle against the carnal self, and they were in continuous spiritual contact with the Creator in their worship and daily lives. They were in such a state of submission and worship that others may have thought this was the only pursuit of their lives, but the fact is that Islam was their way of life and they carried out the other aspects of life according to their faith.

The Companions performed every action in their lives with the sole intention of pleasing the Creator; they were the embodiment of the foundation of piety. Umar was one of the finest examples of this; one day he interrupted his own sermon, saying *"O, Umar, you were once a shepherd."* When he left the pulpit the congregation asked him why he said such a thing, he replied, *"I remembered that I am now a Caliph…"*

Another time, Umar was carrying a heavy sack and someone asked him why he was not having someone else carry it and he replied: *"I have a sense of pride in my soul and I am carrying the sack to destroy this pride."*

53

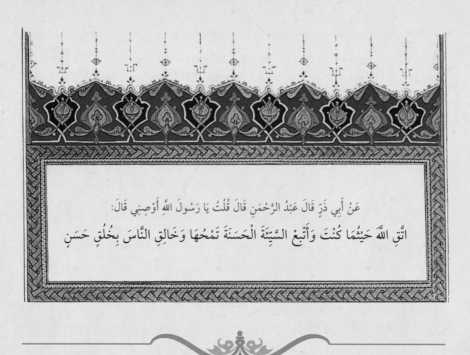

عَنْ أَبِي ذَرٍ قَالَ قَالَ عَبْدُ الرَّحْمَنِ قَالَ قُلْتُ يَا رَسُولَ اللهِ أَوْصِنِي قَالَ:

اتَّقِ اللهَ حَيْثُمَا كُنْتَ وَأَتْبِعْ السَّيِّئَةَ الْحَسَنَةَ تَمْحُهَا وَخَالِقِ النَّاسَ بِخُلُقٍ حَسَنٍ

(17)

PIETY, KINDNESS AND GOOD BEHAVIOR

*"Fear God wherever you are. Follow up a bad deed with
a good deed and it will blot out the former. And deal
with people in good manners."*

(Tirmidhi, Birr, 55; Ahmad ibn Hanbal, Musnad, 5:153)

There is nothing like good manners to exalt one. Good behavior is a virtue of God and a good-mannered person is one who has been blessed with the virtues of the Creator. The above hadith explains the path to piety and the concept of protecting piety in our everyday lives; it is such a vast subject that it would take many books to rightfully illustrate its true significance.

Taqwa is the Arabic word for piety, and means duly fearing God, while pious people are called *Muttaqi*; the guide for these people of wisdom is to live within the boundaries and regulations set by God and Prophet Mu-

54

hammad, peace and blessings be upon him, to live in moderation, avoiding both excess and deficiency. *Taqwa*, like any other action in the life of a believer, must be a guide in the right direction; as in everything else, a Muslim should keep a balanced line at *taqwa*. Setting up difficult principles beyond the frame of the tradition of the Messenger of God and pushing others to practice them means going beyond the boundaries of religion.

To elaborate on this point, one should avoid forcibly imposing supererogatory prayers in addition to the prescribed obligatory prayers; rather, they should stress the significance and merits of optional worship and encourage others about it. For example, we may consider that the night prayer is necessary, because it is the path to seeking God's pleasure, the way to Paradise, and an enlightenment of the soul. This is why in the darkness of the night we stand before the Creator of all when we are alone. At the same time, one should not forget the importance of continuously remembering the Creator and glorifying the One Who has granted us so many blessings in the world. In fact, this constant flow of benevolence and grace that God has bestowed upon us deserves gratitude and thankfulness in our words, actions and behavior; if we were to refrain from showing gratitude and instead ignored the blessings that the Creator has sent us then we might be subjected to Divine punishment. This is stated in the following verse from the Qur'an: *"If you are thankful (for My favors), I will most certainly give you more; but if you are ungrateful, surely My punishment is severe"* (Ibrahim, 14:7).

This is the reason why the continuance of supererogatory worship, whether it is prayer or expression of gratitude, should be considered to be part of our daily duty. In addition, the words of those who worship devotedly will make it far more understandable and acceptable for others.

Another important aspect of *taqwa* that needs great care and attention is that which is permissible and that which is forbidden according to Islam; those who ignore the restrictions or live without taking care will never reach the truth of piety. When they read the Qur'an they will not be able to realize its importance or the invigoration its verses invokes in the human soul. This divine book is the path to piety; a book which has guided pious ones to faith. The principle characteristic of a pious person is that they avoid that which is forbidden and fulfill the obligatory aspects of faith.

It is possible to say that a person's perception of the world plays a great role in reaching true piety; the world motivates human beings in two directions, towards good or towards evil. The Prophet said: *"The world is like a prison for a believer and Paradise for the unbelievers.*" Human beings come in this world once and they see the fruits of their worldly life displayed before them in the Hereafter. This is why acknowledging the real value of the blessings in this world, our youth, health, wealth, and life and utilizing these blessings in the best possible way is necessary; these blessings are the means of gaining everything we require in both this world and the Hereafter.

Of course, there are many unfortunate people who, despite having everything, are blind to the true value of the blessings that have been bestowed upon them; they are like fish living in the ocean, unaware of the true value of the sea until they are swept onto the beach. A human being must live in this world and, regardless of all else, must have a constant awareness of the eternal life of the Hereafter.

Another significant point in acquiring *taqwa* or reaching a new dimension in the scope of *taqwa* is retreating from the routine duties of daily life and occupying ourselves with activities that spiritually intensify human contemplation. We should also feed our minds with relevant reading and return to our duties with refreshed vigor and work efficiently. Organizing such spiritual gatherings and spending time for them are vital dynamics for our life in both worlds, irreplaceable by anything else.

The following verse from Qur'an expresses another characteristic of those who reach true piety, telling us that they are those who:

> *Remember and mention God (with their tongues and hearts), standing and sitting and lying down on their sides (whether during the Prayer or not), and reflect on the creation of the heavens and the earth. (Having grasped the purpose of their creation and the meaning they contain, they conclude and say): "Our Lord, You have not created this (the universe) without meaning and purpose. All-Glorified are You (in that You are absolutely above doing anything meaningless and purposeless), so save us from (having wrong conceptions of Your acts and acting against Your purpose for creation, and so deserving) the punishment of the Fire! Our Lord! Whomever You admit into the Fire, indeed You have brought him to disgrace. (Having concealed or rejected God's signs in the heavens and on the earth, and so denied God or fallen into associating partners with Him,) the wrongdoers will have no helpers (against the Fire). Our Lord! Indeed We have heard a caller calling to faith, saying: 'Believe in your Lord!', so we did believe. Our Lord, forgive us, then, our sins, and blot out from us our evil deeds, and take us to You in death in the company of the truly godly and virtuous. Our Lord! Grant us what You have promised us through Your Messengers. Do not disgrace us on the Day of Resurrection; indeed You never break Your promise. (Al-Imran 3:191-194)*

عَنْ أَبِي بَكْرَةَ قَالَ قَالَ رَسُولُ اللهِ صَلَّى اللهُ عَلَيْهِ وَسَلَّمَ:

كَمَا تَكُونُوا يُوَلَّى عَلَيْكُمْ

(18)

SOCIETY AND ADMINISTRATION

"You are governed according to how you are."

(Daylami, Musnad, 3:305)

How a nation is governed is reflected on the citizens. A leader's principles are the source of the society's principles. According to the principle stated in another hadith: *"Each of you is a shepherd and each of you is responsible for what you tend,"* everybody has their own responsibilities, including leaders of communities and nations. The difference is that leaders are responsible not only for leading the community, but also for how they administer; however, if we look at the statement: *"You are governed according to how you are."* this adds a totally new dimension to the laws and regulations of society.

First, the hadith expresses the importance of administration, for it clearly reminds leaders that they will be accountable for the actions of the community; that is, they are responsible for guiding the community. Society has its own guidelines and policies, just as physics, chemistry and astronomy have their own established rules and regulations, which we call the "laws of nature." These social principles and rules will continue until the Judgment Day. It is for this reason that human beings are constantly dragged into evil and bad actions; if a society is given a life of evil then they are bound to be guided by evil. This is an invariable aspect of Divine law. If evil flourishes within a society, then God provides them with rulers of the same qualities.

Another point we can also infer from this hadith is that, laws and regulations are things written on paper after all, even if people exert themselves to prepare the soundest of laws. The important point here is whether people abide by the principles they contain. In other words, what really matters is the ethical stance of the people governed; if they have good ethical conduct on their part, the people to govern them will not be problematic.

At this point, it will be appropriate to give an example from history. During the rule of Hajjaj the Cruel, one man mentioned to him the justice during the caliphate of Umar ibn al-Khattab. Hajjaj replied that had they been like the people during the time of Umar, he would surely be like Umar.

A third aspect is that everybody must always seek out their own faults. If people try to whitewash their own egos and seek other causes to blame, they cannot make progress in the real sense. As it is declared in the Qur'an, God Almighty does not change the condition of a people unless they change themselves within (Ra'd 13:11). Corruption in one unit will surely be reflected in all units, including the upper levels. This is also true for individuals' ethical conduct. So the fact that the condition of those will be reflected in the condition of those who govern them is expressed by the Prophet with a succinct statement, as in all his sayings.

عَنْ عُمَرَ بْنِ الْخَطَّابِ رَضِيَ اللهُ عَنْهُ يَقُولُ قَالَ رَسُولَ اللهِ صَلَّى اللهُ عَلَيْهِ وَسَلَّمَ:
إِنَّمَا الْأَعْمَالُ بِالنِّيَّاتِ وَإِنَّمَا لِكُلِّ امْرِئٍ مَا نَوَى فَمَنْ كَانَتْ هِجْرَتُهُ إِلَى اللهِ
وَرَسُولِهِ فَهِجْرَتُهُ إِلَى اللهِ وَرَسُولِهِ وَمَنْ كَانَتْ هِجْرَتُهُ لِدُنْيَا يُصِيبُهَا أَوْ امْرَأَةٍ
يَتَزَوَّجُهَا فَهِجْرَتُهُ إِلَى مَا هَاجَرَ إِلَيْهِ

(19)

DEEDS ARE TO BE JUDGED
ACCORDING TO INTENTIONS

"Deeds are judged by their intentions and every man shall have only that
which he intended. The migration of those who migrated for the sake
of God and His Messenger was for God and his Messenger, while the
migration of one whose migration was to achieve some worldly benefit or
to take someone in marriage was for that which he migrated."

(Muslim, Imara, 155; Abu Dawud, Talaq, 10)

The prime topic of this hadith is the migration, and it was uttered in connection with the following incident: During the period when everyone began migrating from Mecca to Medina in the hope of obtaining the pleasure of the Creator, one of the Companions, migrated to be with a woman he loved dearly called Umm Qays. This Companion without doubt was a devoted and faithful man, but the motive of his migration was his intention for marriage.

He had also migrated, but for the sake of the woman he loved, he bore great difficulties and hardships that should only be endued for the sake of God and this is reflected in the hadith. The hadith is not just a comment aimed at a particular subject; rather it is a ruling that is concerned with every aspect of a person's life.

Everybody is rewarded according to the intention of their act; if they immigrate for the sake of God and his Messenger, then they will be rewarded accordingly. This is also the case with praying, fasting and giving charitable alms. Those who seek merit and grace from the Creator will be constantly rewarded with the compassion, kindness, and beneficence of the Almighty.

When a human being reaches this level of compassion they will persist in increasing their affection and relationship by prostrating before their Creator, totally overwhelmed with joy, excitement and aspiration. As they become closer to their Lord, this enthusiasm and emotion will prevail over every action. When one surpasses the universe they will stand before the Creator wherever they go, be it in the grave, in the abode of torment, on the Day of Judgment or on the bridge that stretches over hellfire. If a person's actions are successful in reaching the *Liva al-Hamd*[15] they will encounter the Prophet of the Universe, an event that is beyond anything they could ever imagine.

If the sole intention of a person is not the the quest for Divine pleasure, any difficulty they endure will be in vain; if their intention to migrate was to be with the woman they loved then they suffer hardship and adversity for the material pleasures of this life. A person who ignores the voice that emerges deep from their soul, the emotions of their conscience, a person who lives for the pleasures of the world and wastes their life seeking enjoy-

---

[15] The Prophet's Flag, around which Muslims will gather on the Judgment Day.

ment wherever possible will never prosper or obtain the pleasures of those whose every action is carefully calculated to please their Creator.

In another hadith the Prophet says that the intention of a believer is more important than his deed. However great an effort one exerts it is nearly impossible to have one's actions match the sincerity of their intentions, but the Creator of great compassion rewards a person according to the sincere intention of their soul, not their actions. Thus, it is quite clear that a believer's intentions are a greater advantage than their physical actions.

I would like to focus on another hadith that is related to the same subject: "*Indeed, there is in the body a piece of flesh which if it is sound then the whole body is sound and if it is corrupt then the whole body is corrupt. Indeed it is the heart*" (Bukhari, Iman, 39). If a believer is sincere in their soul, then every seed of prosperity they sow in life will mature and then flourish into branches of benevolence. These branches will be their shade on the Day of Judgment. The seeds sown with sincerity of heart will grow in prosperity and appear before us on the Day of Questioning in the form of the benevolent fruits of Paradise.

The ordinary chores of a Muslim's daily life are transformed into acts of worship through good intentions; every single breath of the believer who sleeps with the intention of waking for prayer during the night will be considered as a part of their worship. If we consider our lifespan on this earth, how could we possibly attain Paradise in such a short span of time? Because of our intention of eternal servitude to God, believers are blessed with admittance into the gardens of Paradise, whereas disbelievers are doomed by their intention of eternal ungratefulness.

Good intentions, ranging from the most insignificant to the greatest of actions, are the only aspect that enhances the true value and worthiness of human life in this world and the rewards in the Hereafter. The intention of kindness is a great benefit in this life. If a person has the intention of evil in their soul, but refrains from performing this evil action, they will be rewarded accordingly; however, if the intention of evil remains this is not classed as a sin. Only when this evil action is actually put into practice will it be recorded as one sin. Still, we should not underestimate any sins.

We should not ignore the significance of migration in this hadith. Every believer who leaves his homeland, family, wife and children to convey the truth to others is in a perpetual circle of compassion and, without a doubt, will be rewarded in the Hereafter for their sincere intentions. No specific reward for such great actions has been mentioned; this can be owing to a surprise reward to be granted in the Hereafter.

The definite article in Arabic (al-) at the beginning of the word "deeds" denotes that deeds gain a true value only through intention. No form of worship can be accepted without sincere intention, and therefore if a person continuously prays, fasts, spends of their wealth, performs the rituals of Hajj without the intention to do so in their heart, then their actions are in vain. Prayer, fasting, charity and Hajj are only acceptable forms of worship if a person has a sincere intention in their soul, thus making it the actual intention that transforms actions into worship.

If we take another look at the topic of the hadith, we can see that the Prophet first defined the vast subject of "intention" in three short words, and then with a few sentences he expressed the gist of an important matter like *hijra*—whose meaning covers a wide scope of acts, from abandoning sins to all of the migrations to be realized for the sake of God until the end of the world.

It may be of use to elaborate on this with another hadith: *"The greatest muhajir (emigrant) is he who abandons sin"* (Nasai, Iman, 9) One day Ibrahim ibn Adham prayed to his Lord: *"O Lord! With Your love in my heart, I have forsaken everything and come to You. After finding You, I do not see anything else wherever I look."* At a time when his soul was so full of spiritual emotion Ibrahim ibn Adham saw his son next to the Kaʿba. When the young man recognized his father they ran to each other in a state of elation and embraced one another. Just then Ibrahim heard a voice saying: *"O Ibrahim, there cannot be two objects of love in one heart"* and Ibrahim started praying: *"O God, take from me what prevents Your love,"* and his son instantly dropped dead.

Avoiding the sins and evil in this world and turning to the Creator in a state of repentance, asking forgiveness until one's prayers are accepted by the Almighty is a form of *hijra* which has been beautifully expressed in the following prayer:

> *"O God, Your sinful servant stands before You. Seeking Your forgiveness,*
> *professing his sins and begging to be forgiven.*
> *If You grant forgiveness, this is out of Your glory.*
> *And if You dismiss him, there is no one else to show mercy."*

A person who abandons their past sins and acknowledges that the repetition of these sins deserves a punishment that is greater than the fire of hell is on the true path of *hijra*. Those who avoid the forbidden boundaries of Islam, perceiving it to be like a field of hidden mines waiting to explode, those who refrain from the prohibited aspects of religion with their actions and speech, continuing to perform a holy migration throughout their lives, whether they are among others or in seclusion, maintain the emotion of hijra in their souls.

Nevertheless, seclusion is another distinct aspect of hijra, for this is where devoted believers reach a true understanding of divinity.

We can examine the main subjects and explanations of this hadith as follows:

a- Intention is the spirit of any action; actions with no intention have no significance.

b- Intention is the light of spirituality which turns evil into good and good into evil.

c- A person's actions are transformed into good deeds with intentions, thus hijra with no sincere intention would be a migration of no importance, Hajj a deceptive journey, prayer a routine of physical action and fasting nothing more than abstinence. Pure intention of the soul is the only possible way to convert these actions into good deeds and forms of worship that will lead us to the gates of Paradise.

d- Eternal Paradise is the result of the sincere intention of eternal servitude, whereas the eternal flames of hell are the consequence of eternal denial and blasphemy.

e- A minimal degree of effort opens the doors of opportunity. A believer can achieve rewards of great value both for this world and the Hereafter simply with the sincere intention of the soul.

f- Those who know the value of sincere intention in the sight of God will be in a position to aspire great achievements.

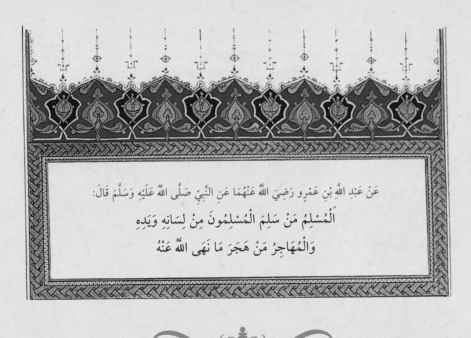

عَنْ عَبْدِ اللهِ بْنِ عَمْرٍو رَضِيَ اللهُ عَنْهُمَا عَنِ النَّبِيِّ صَلَّى اللهُ عَلَيْهِ وَسَلَّمَ قَالَ:
الْمُسْلِمُ مَنْ سَلِمَ الْمُسْلِمُونَ مِنْ لِسَانِهِ وَيَدِهِ
وَالْمُهَاجِرُ مَنْ هَجَرَ مَا نَهَى اللهُ عَنْهُ

AN IDEAL MUSLIM AND THE EVIL OF
THE TONGUE AND HAND

"A true Muslim is the one from whose tongue and hands
Muslims are safe. And a Muhajir (emigrant) is the one who
abandons all that God has forbidden."

(Bukhari, Iman, 4; Abu Dawud, Jihad, 2)

The use of the Arabic definite article at the beginning of the phrases "Muslim" and "Muslims" denotes a special meaning. They actually refer to ideal Muslims, the sincere devoted believers who abstain from evil actions, who have totally absorbed themselves in an atmosphere of security and salvation. These people are totally different to those who claim to be believers or Muslims just because they were born into Muslim families. Their entire way of life portrays the idealistic sincerity of a true believer. Their thoughts and actions are a conveyance of perfection; therefore, when one says "a sincere believer," the first person who comes to mind is a Muslim of perfection. This is the description of the Muslim portrayed in this hadith.

Besides the main topic of the hadith, one thing to be noted here is the language use.

Under normal circumstances, only a learned person taught by an expert knows such fine points of language. It is known that there was no question of such education for the Prophet of God; he was blessed with the ability of speech and preached that which the Almighty Creator taught him. This is why the teachings and expressions of Prophet Muhammad were conveyed in a manner of speech that was free from any kind of defect.

Again, if we turn to the contents of the hadith, a true Muslim is a figure of reliance and trust. This is true to such an extent that other Muslims attain a sense of security and unlimited confidence, having no doubts in the sincerity of such people and completely seeing them as trustworthy. To such people they entrust their families, the dearest and most valuable existence of their lives, with total assurance that no harm will befall them. Following a meeting or conversation with these people you feel a sense of security; you know these believers would neither gossip about you nor disclose secrets to others; indeed, they would even prevent others from doing so. Such a person approaches others with the same sensitivity and respect for their dignity as if it were their own honor that is in question; they feed and provide for others before themselves and dedicate to working for the benefit of those around them. This is just a short explanation of the vast qualities that the sincere believers mentioned in this hadith have.

A believer gives greetings to both those they are acquainted with and to complete strangers; such behavior sows the seeds of friendship and love in the soul (Bukhari, Muslim). On completion of the prayer the true believer's greetings are accepted by all of existence, from the angels to the spirits; they bestow good tidings on both the apparent and the unseen; this is behavior that Muslims of sincerity perform and it is one that has never been conveyed to such an extent by others throughout history.

A person enters Islam adhering to the prayer, fasting, performing the Hajj and witnessing the unification of the Creator as commanded in the Qur'an *"O you who believe! Come in full submission to God, all of you…"* (Baqara

2:208). This means opening the soul to the vast ocean of bliss and contentment; nothing but goodness is expected from a person in this state.

Every word in this hadith is chosen with great care, as in all other sayings of the Prophet. There are, of course, many reasons for focusing on hand and tongue. There are two ways of harming those around us. We can cause others harm either directly or behind their back. Direct damage to humans is through actions; indirect damage is caused to one who is not present via the tongue, or in other words, with speech. A human can either violate the rights of others by assaulting them or violate the rights of others in their absence by gossiping and undermining their reputation and dignity. Both are immoral acts never to be performed by a sincere Muslim; a sincere Muslim acts benevolently toward others, whether it is directly or in their absence.

The Prophet mentioned the tongue, or speech, before the hand (actions). It is quite possible that there is the potential of reaction or retaliation when a deed is physical, whereas in case of gossip or slander, the response often remains unchallenged. Therefore, there is an ever-present possibility that a person could vilify another person, their environment or even cause a conflict between nations.

Defending oneself against harms to be done by tongue is much more difficult than defense against direct physical abuse, and it is for this reason that Prophet Muhammad mentioned speech before physical actions. Also, this demonstrates the importance of the values we have been given by God; in fact, protecting the dignity and reputation of other Muslims is so important that a believer is commanded to control both their tongue and hands.

One of the important moral concepts of Islam, which came with a universal notion of security and well-being, is a Muslim individual's refraining from harmful things, whereas Islam's other aspect is to ensure that no harm will befall others. Thus, a Muslim as an individual should distance themselves from affairs that could cause harm to both him and others; this is of great importance as it is not only the means of refraining from harming others, but it actually provides assurance and instills confidence in every sector and layer of society.

A true believer has a feeling of security in his or her heart. Such people inspire a feeling of security everywhere they go. They greet other believers with wishes of peace for when they come and leave. During *salat* they wish peace for all the righteous servants and they finish by greeting the angels on both sides. It would be unthinkable that a human who continues to live within this constant circle of well wishing could wander from the path of truth, a path that ensures well being, spiritually and/or materially, for humans in this world and the Hereafter, or unthinkable will be for them to participate in anything that would result in harm to them as an individual or cause harm to others.

Following these initial remarks in relation to the hadith, we can continue to explore these aspects that have great spirituality:

a- A sincere Muslim is the most reliable representative of universal peace on the earth.

b- A Muslim conveys the intense emotions experienced deep in their soul wherever they go.

c- A Muslim is perceived as the symbol of security and kindness, who never causes harm or distress to others.

d- A Muslim considers verbal abuse to be equal to physical abuse; namely gossip, slander and insult. Indeed, in many cases these can be a greater sin than physical abuse.

e- According to our faith, even if a believer perpetrates any of these evil sins they remain a Muslim; this is not a topic that delineates between blasphemy and belief.

f- As in every matter, a believer should have a broad horizon in matters of faith and the practice of Islam; they should not be content as ordinary Muslims but intend for perfection in faith. The above mentioned ones and even further meanings are included within the pithy statement of the Messenger of God.

عَنْ أَبِي هُرَيْرَةَ قَالَ قَالَ رَسُولُ اللهِ صَلَّى اللهُ عَلَيْهِ وَسَلَّمَ:
مِنْ حُسْنِ إِسْلَامِ الْمَرْءِ تَرْكُهُ مَا لَا يَعْنِيهِ

ABANDONING THAT WHICH IS OF NO BENEFIT

*"Abandoning that which is of no benefit results from a
person's practicing Islam beautifully."*

(Tirmidhi, Zuhd, 11; Ibn Maja, Fitan, 12)

Of course, it is nearly impossible to fully understand the true depths and spiritual scope of Prophet Muhammad's words of wisdom from just a literal translation. The hadith relates the mystery of a believer's achieving soundness of faith. This is a Muslim who has reached a degree of perfection on the outside as well as assimilating which in their soul the mystery of *ihsan*—perfect goodness, or the level of faith where a believer worships with the consciousness of seeing God or being seen by Him. Such people will—and should—abandon whatever is of no use to them.

People who lack in seriousness have the same problem in their worship and religious duties. When a person like this stands before the His Glory in worship they may seem genuinely devout, nevertheless, if their soul and conscience have not reached genuine devotion, then their actions are nothing but affectation. However, a person's true character cannot be hidden forever; one day the true morals are sure to become apparent, if, of course, affectation has not become the overriding characteristic of this person's life. Such an attitude requires a great deal of effort, but eventually the pretense will be overcome; a person cannot go on pretending to be different from their true characteristics for very long. Whatever we do, there is no escape from reality. To sum up: there should be inner profundity so that it is manifested in one's actions. Serious manners should be a manifestation of a person's inner world.

When one of the Companions was recommended for the position of caliph, Umar ibn Khattab said: *"This person is worthy of the caliphate in every way, but he jokes too much; a position like this requires gravity."* Given that being a "caliph" in the sense of ruling over others requires gravity, it definitely requires gravity in the sense of being God's vicegerent on earth.

The Arabic preposition "min" (from) used in the hadith expresses specification; that is, there is a certain way necessary for a person to achieve the consciousness of *ihsan*. On one occasion, Archangel Gabriel came to Prophet Muhammad, peace and blessings be upon him, and asked what faith is, and then Islam, and after affirming the Prophet's answers, he asked about *ihsan*. The Messenger of God replied: *"Ihsan is your worshipping God as if you were seeing Him. Even though you do not, He sees you"* (Bukhari, Tawhid, 35). Here, Gabriel's asking about *ihsan* as the final question shows that *ihsan* is taken as the final level of faith.

This degree of belief can only be achieved with true piety (*taqwa*), asceticism and saintly wisdom; one should first take achieving *ihsan* as an ideal, and then continue to follow the paths of prosperity that leads to such a degree of faith. God is closer to human beings than the jugular vein. The whole of creation exists due to the power of the Almighty; seeking the Creator elsewhere is in vain. He is closer to us than we are to ourselves. Full awareness of this mystery is *ihsan*. When such awareness dominates the conscience, their behaviors become a manifestation of firm faith. God loves firmness of good deeds. He declares in the Qur'an as follows:

> Say: "Work, and God will see your work, and so will His Messenger and the true believers; and you will be brought back to the Knower of the Unseen (of all that lies beyond sense-perception) and the witnessed (the sensed realm), and He will make you understand all that you were doing (and call you to account for it)" (Tawba, 9:105).

Thus, Muslims must perform every action with total awareness that their actions will be inspected by the Creator, His Prophet, and true believers as mentioned in the verse. Therefore, every action must be carried out appropriately with awareness that this will occur, so that when that day eventually does come we will not be humiliated; and this can only be achieved through *ihsan*. Individuals with the ability to attain such profundity with respect to their inner worlds will present perfected behaviors and will have nothing to do with anything unseemly. Thus, by becoming a person of perfection will achieve the excellence of Islam.

The Arabic phrase *"ma la yanih"* used in the hadith expresses a person's being engaged in actions, which have no virtue or benefit neither presently nor in the future. Such activities are just time wasting actions that have no real benefit for the individual, their family, or nation. A person of faith who achieves the excellence of Islam avoids such behavior; therefore, this hadith is teaching us to occupy ourselves with affairs that are of benefit to all. In a way, this defines the meaning of being an earnest person.

At this point we should underline another subtle aspect of the hadith. People preoccupied with trivial matters will not have the opportunity to exert themselves with matters that truly concern them; they will never find the time to concentrate on directing their actions and thoughts to necessary subjects.

It is impossible for a person who does not know right from wrong to choose the true path of guidance; a person who is engaged in unnecessary affairs will never be able to be engaged in lofty and sensible pursuits.

عَنْ أَنَسِ بْنِ مَالِكٍ رَضِيَ اللهُ عَنْهُ قَالَ:

مَرَّ النَّبِيُّ صَلَّى اللهُ عَلَيْهِ وَسَلَّمَ بِامْرَأَةٍ تَبْكِي عِنْدَ قَبْرٍ فَقَالَ اتَّقِي اللهَ وَاصْبِرِي

قَالَتْ إِلَيْكَ عَنِّي فَإِنَّكَ لَمْ تُصَبْ بِمُصِيبَتِي وَلَمْ تَعْرِفْهُ فَقِيلَ لَهَا إِنَّهُ النَّبِيُّ

صَلَّى اللهُ عَلَيْهِ وَسَلَّمَ فَأَتَتْ بَابَ النَّبِيِّ صَلَّى اللهُ عَلَيْهِ وَسَلَّمَ فَلَمْ تَجِدْ عِنْدَهُ

بَوَّابِينَ فَقَالَتْ لَمْ أَعْرِفْكَ فَقَالَ إِنَّمَا الصَّبْرُ عِنْدَ الصَّدْمَةِ الْأُولَى

SHOWING PATIENCE

"The Prophet passed by a woman who was wailing beside a grave. He told her to fear God and be patient. She said to him: 'Go away, for you have not been afflicted with a calamity like mine.' She did not recognize him. Then she was informed that the man she had spoken to was the Prophet. She went to the house of the Prophet and there she did not find any guard. Then she apologized from him saying, 'I did not recognize you.' He said, 'Verily, patience is at the first stroke (of a calamity).'"

(Bukhari, Janaiz, 32; Muslim, Janaiz, 14–15)

When Prophet Muhammad realized that some of the customs from the pre-Islamic period of ignorance were continuing, he prohibited Muslims from visiting the graves. This restriction was later lifted and the Prophet encouraged his followers to visit graves, telling them: *"I forbade you to visit the graves but (now) visit them!"* (Bukhari, Iman, 37). There is a point in visiting the graves because this is where the most influential lesson of salvation from worldly desires is revealed. The Prophet would pay frequent visits to graves and made a habit of visiting the graves of the martyrs of the Battle of Uhud at least once a week.

On one of his visits to the graveyard the Prophet noticed a woman sitting beside a grave crying, wailing and tearing her clothes. He approached the woman to calm her down and give her advice, but the woman did not recognize Prophet Muhammad and said: *"Go away, for you have not been afflicted with a calamity like mine."* Prophet Muhammad left without saying anything; then those witnessed the event told her that the person she had spoken to had been the Prophet.

She was shocked, sad and very ashamed, for she had unintentionally been rude to the Messenger of God. The woman ran to the Prophet's house and entered, without even knocking on the door, and apologized to him. The Prophet Muhammad replied: *"Verily patience is at the first stroke of calamity."* These few short words of wisdom were of great significance; the Prophet referred to a topic to be covered in entire books with wondrous eloquence. There are a few different kinds of patience, such as patience in tribulation, patience in resisting evil and patience in the perseverance of worship.

The Arabic name of a bitter plant (*sabir*) is derived from the same root with the word patience (*sabr*). This curative herb is said to have a very bitter taste. So showing patience is bitter just like swallowing this bitter cure. However, enduring the initial bitterness has always given sweet results.

Of course patience, showing tolerance, determination, remaining calm and enduring distressful events is not an easy task. Nevertheless, this is something that should be done at the initial shock of a disaster; psychologically, change of position and condition will relieve grief and help a person to forget the hardship and sorrow caused by such a calamity.

It is at the first blow, although the calamity may seem unbearable, that a person should make an effort to overcome the initial shock. We can try to do this by physically changing our position. For instance, if we are standing we can sit down, if we are sitting we can lie down or we can change the form of activity we are doing. This can be achieved by making ablutions, praying, distancing oneself from the topic of a conversation regarding the subject... a change of environment or even sleeping will contribute to easing the initial shock. Any similar changes can help break the state of shock and lessen the impact of the calamity to a certain extent.

Every difficulty presents some kind of trauma and when the initial shock fades this can be transformed into compassion, distress becomes joy and grief contentment; therefore, if a person successfully overcomes the initial shock the emotion of grief and sorrow in the soul will be replaced by contentment and acceptance; this is the intricate topic that was expressed by Prophet Muhammad, peace and blessings be upon him, in a few short words.

Patience, in the sense of keeping steadfast, is a requirement for the continuation of worship and other religious duties as well; initially when a person begins to pray or perform any other form of worship it may be difficult, but if they are patient and continue with spiritual awareness and feelings, then abandoning these duties, including fasting, giving to charity and performing the Hajj, as well as the obligatory prayers, will eventually cause distress and generate a constant sense of anguish deep in the soul.

Think of the blessed people who perform the Hajj under such difficult conditions, yet they have a constant yearning in their souls to visit the holy land and enhance their spiritual enlightenment. Such emotions mean that this person has overcome the initial impact of hardship. This is valid for any form of worship; once you start doing them, they become much easier.

A person must show the same patience in resisting against the temptation of sins; the initial resistance shown when we are faced with potential evil or sin eliminates any possibility of harm and ensures that human beings avoid iniquity. This is why Prophet Muhammad told Ali: *"The first look is pardonable, but the second is haram (forbidden)"* (Tirmidhi, Adab, 28). There is always the possibility that looking at someone of the opposite sex can lead to evil, therefore if we avoid the second glance, the first is not classed as a sin. In this way we protect ourselves against evil actions and in turn may even be rewarded for complying with the prohibitions. But a second glance leads to evil thoughts, which in turn causes spiritual decline and decay of the soul. Every time we look at something that is prohibited there is a possibility of straying from the path of purity and participating in evil actions. If a person chooses the path of evil this is the first step on the journey of destruction. Redemption from here is very difficult and it is for this reason that Prophet Muhammad told us with words of wisdom to refrain from evil when the possibility first arises.

Epictetus said: *"When the idea of any pleasure strikes your imagination, make a computation between the duration of the pleasure and that of the repentance that is likely to follow."* This statement conveys such inspiration; if Epictetus had lived after Prophet Muhammad we would surely believe he had actually been inspired by the Prophet's words of wisdom.

A person becomes so accustomed to performing sinful actions that eventually sinning turns into a habit, a bad addiction. Only good actions shed the light of faith into the soul and act as a shield of protection against sin and the flames of hellfire; in time, avoiding sin becomes a part of a person's nature and when they encounter evil they reach into the depths of their soul. The essence of spirituality leads one into an atmosphere of morality and ensures that anything which could cause harm to the soul is avoided.

عَنْ شَدَّادٍ قَالَ سَمِعْتُ أَبَا أُمَامَةَ قَالَ قَالَ رَسُولُ اللهِ صَلَّى اللهُ عَلَيْهِ وَسَلَّمَ:
يَا ابْنَ آدَمَ إِنَّكَ أَنْ تَبْذُلَ الْفَضْلَ خَيْرٌ لَكَ وَأَنْ تُمْسِكَهُ شَرٌّ لَكَ وَلَا تُلَامُ عَلَى
كَفَافٍ وَابْدَأْ بِمَنْ تَعُولُ وَالْيَدُ الْعُلْيَا خَيْرٌ مِنَ الْيَدِ السُّفْلَى

23

THE HAND THAT GIVES IS SUPERIOR
TO THE ONE THAT TAKES

"O son of Adam, it is better for you if you spend your surplus (wealth), but if you withhold it, it is evil for you. There is (however) no reproach for you (if you withhold the means necessary) for a living. And begin (charity) with your dependents and those close to you; the upper hand (giving hand) is better than the lower hand (taking hand)."

(Bukhari, Zakat, 18; Muslim, Zakat, 97)

This topic of giving in charity was mentioned in another hadith (Bukhari, *Zakat* 18), and it is made clear by the Prophet himself that the upper hand is the one which gives or donates, and the lower hand is the one which receives. In addition to the idea that the hand that gives is superior to the hand that takes, the hadith is stating that the hand which gives charity will be superior in terms of virtue and being rewarded in the Hereafter. Therefore, from the point of human honor and dignity, the hand that gives represents "loftiness," and the other represents "lowliness." Such perfectly chosen words encourage charity, and at the same time discourage receiving unless one really has to. In order to fulfill the duty of giving alms there must be a receiver, a person in need, to actually accept the charity. The hadith is adequate to say that the giving hand is better, without remarking that "the receiving hand is evil." Instead, it is implied that the receiving hand is lesser in goodness while at the same time reminds the fact that receiving is permissible under certain conditions.

Although the above meanings can be inferred from the hadith, it will be inadequate to translate it as "the giving hand is superior than the receiving hand," since the original hadith is not phrased this way. The Noble Prophet tended to give preference to metaphorical statements. Therefore interpreting the relevant terms as the "giving hand" and the "receiving hand" can only reflect one of the meanings but it certainly does not reflect the entire meaning.

Firstly, we see here a figure of speech known as synecdoche, in which a part represents the whole. That is, "the hand" refers to the individual. Thus, we can also infer the meaning that *The person who gives is better than the person who takes.*

Secondly, in Arabic, the word *al-muʿti* refers to the giver while *al-aahidh* refers to the receiver. If the Prophet had used these words as adjectives to the word "hand," then it would have been appropriate to say *the hand that provides is more benevolent than the hand that receives.* However, the Prophet does not mention a *giving hand* or a *receiving hand.* Instead, he mentions an *upper* and a *lower* hand. This brings us to the following point: the giving hand is not always necessarily of greater virtue in comparison to the one who receives; the receiver of charity may have—even though not with great difference—an upper and better hand in some instances: when the receiver is obliged to take, or is taking with the intention to make the other give to charity, or when the giver mentions the favor in a way to embarrass the receiver. In such cases, even though the giving hand seems to have an upper level, it is below the latter to a certain extent in reality.

There are poor but thankful people whom the Prophet refers to as *fuqara al-sabirin*—the patient poor. Such people are usually treated as

76

objects of scorn. However, as stated by the Prophet, if they swear that a certain thing will happen, God does not make them wrong in their word. Bara Ibn Malik was one such person. When the Muslims had great difficulty in battle, they would appeal to Bara Ibn Malik to swear that they would win. After he swore, they would really emerge victorious (Ibn Hajar, *al-Isaba*, 1:143). So the receiving hand can sometimes be such a blessed person's.

Another of the poverty stricken Companions was Sawban; he followed the Prophet's advice to not ask for anything from others; he complied with the Messenger's words to such an extent that when his whip fell to the ground he dismounted from his camel and picked up the whip himself so that he would not have to ask anyone to give it to him (Ibn Hajar, *al-Isaba*, 1:143). Thus, giving to such people can be compared to giving to an angel; these are the individuals who are in no way inferior to the providers. We understand from another hadith reported by Aisha that, when we give charity to such people, we virtually hand what we give directly to the Almighty Creator, and what is given is directly handed to the receiver by the Almighty Creator (Bukhari, Zakat, 8).

With these words of wisdom the Prophet is actually advising us: "*Always maintain your dignity. Never denigrate your soul by begging or by declining to be those who receive (charity) as individuals or as a nation. Constantly try to guard your position of being the hand that gives. In this way you will constantly guard your honor and be indignant. Never forget the superior will always give of wealth with confidence while the lower collects and lives with constant worry. So have the dominant hand and not the dependant. If you have the upper hand, you will prevail.*"

These words are an important guide for human beings regarding international relations; making a concerted effort to have the upper hand will bring a certain international status. This is how a people can find a chance to avoid being exploited. Otherwise, they will remain as people of contempt and dishonor; the clearest evidence of this is what we see around us at the present. We are all suffering the consequences of being at the hand of dependence; some wealthy nations provide ostensible financial support to governments that are less fortunate, and then exploit them in every way, taking much more than they originally give. In conclusion, individuals and societies are supposed to work, strive, and display a performance which results in human dignity.

عَنْ أَبِي ذَرٍّ عَنِ النَّبِيِّ صَلَّى اللهُ عَلَيْهِ وَسَلَّمَ قَالَ:

ثَلَاثَةٌ لَا يُكَلِّمُهُمُ اللهُ يَوْمَ الْقِيَامَةِ وَلَا يَنْظُرُ إِلَيْهِمْ وَلَا يُزَكِّيهِمْ وَلَهُمْ عَذَابٌ أَلِيمٌ قَالَ
فَقَرَأَهَا رَسُولُ اللهِ صَلَّى اللهُ عَلَيْهِ وَسَلَّمَ ثَلَاثَ مِرَارًا قَالَ أَبُو ذَرٍّ خَابُوا وَخَسِرُوا
مَنْ هُمْ يَا رَسُولَ اللهِ قَالَ الْمُسْبِلُ وَالْمَنَّانُ وَالْمُنْفِقُ سِلْعَتَهُ بِالْحَلِفِ الْكَاذِبِ

24

THE THREE CLASSES OF PEOPLE WHO
WILL BE SHOWN NO FAVOR

"There are three classes (of people) to whom God will not speak on the Day of Judgment nor will He look at them or redeem them." The Prophet repeated this three times. Abu Dharr said: "O, they are lost and ruined. Who are they, Messenger of God?" Prophet Muhammad said: "Those who trail their robes (arrogant ones), those who put others under obligation by mentioning the favor they made to them, and those who try to market their goods by false swearing."

(Muslim, Iman, 171)

78

The "three" (translated here as "three classes of people") mentioned in this hadith are undetermined; these could consist of individuals or groups, they could be male or female, or they could be from communities of scholars or men of ignorance. What we are interested in here is more the characteristics of these people rather than their identity. Leaving the "three" indefinite means that these people are so worthless and contemptible that it is not even worth giving them a value or defining who they actually are. In the same way that God will neither look nor speak to them, other people will also have no desire to know or speak to them, for their hearts, not their appearances, are at fault. Their souls have been trapped deep within the body with no ability or intention in any way to reach a position of honor and they will continue to struggle in this dungeon of superficiality.

After mentioning these "three," the three verbs follow up (paraphrased into sentences in translation), which reveal the three ways in which a person will be subjected to the punishment of the Creator. These three verbs present a grim picture for the three classes of people mentioned; as the verbs are used in *mudari* case which indicates present and future time, one feels as if watching the unfortunate end of those three classes.

The first way they will be punished is that *"God will not speak to them."* The disaster begins with this first sentence. In Surah Rahman of the Qur'an God the Merciful mentions speech as a blessing. Although humanity is honored with a manifestation of divine speech, the people mentioned in the hadith fall into such a condition that God will not heed them.

What greater punishment could there possibly be than being ignored by the Creator at a time when we most need to speak or beg for divine forgiveness? We stand before the Creator, pleading for Divine mercy; but the only being that could possibly embrace us with compassion and mercy at this time of great despair turns away from us, ignoring our pleas. The Qur'an reveals that God will say: *"Away with you into it! No longer address Me!"* (Al-Muminun 23:108). Here, we are being informed that the place for humans to speak and confer with their Creator is the universe, therefore we should take the opportunity to speak and plead with Almighty in the world of mortality; for if they did not seek refuge in God in the world, He will not be their guardian in the Hereafter.

79

The second punishment is that "*God will not look at them*" on the Day of Judgment; at a time when people are in the greatest need of His compassion, God will turn away from them and while some will gain the pleasure of standing before their Creator, others will be dismayed and sink into despair.

While everyone is being addressed and called by their names, waiting in the hope of salvation, the condition of those who have been rejected will be tragic. Three Companions who failed to join the Tabuk campaign were punished by such rejection for a short period until the revelation declared their forgiveness; this punishment was severe for them. The people mentioned in this hadith are subjected to the same punishment, but for eternity. Being ignored by the Creator, He Who is of eternal compassion, must be one of the worst punishments anyone could endure. People always get what they deserve and nothing less; those who do good will be rewarded with goodness and kindness and those who do evil will be exposed to evil.

The third punishment is that "*God will not redeem them*," or "purify" them to be exact. A person must be cleansed of sin or any kind of evil in this world and go before their Creator in a state of purity. It is only then that All-Forgiving will forgive us for any sins we have committed. The only form of purification in the hereafter is Hell and this is why there is no forgiveness for these people when they stand before God on the Day of Reckoning.

A person is given the opportunity to obtain the pleasures of the Hereafter while they live on the earth; however, when their lives in this world end, so too do their chances of salvation. Therefore, whoever utilizes the opportunity to obtain rewards will be those who gain eternally and those who ignore this chance will undoubtedly be amongst the losers.

With their spiritual faculties inflicted by sins, people will appear before God in a wretched condition and seek for a way to be purified. The Creator will show no mercy in forgiving any of the three categories mentioned above. As declared in the Qur'an, the only thing awaiting them on their departure from this world is a grievous punishment.

So who are those who will be subjected to such a fate? Who are those who will be deprived of God's mercy, whom He will not speak to, nor look at and neither forgive? And who are those who deserve such a grave punishment?

A person who has read the hadith to this point becomes curious about these three groups of individuals. *"Those who trail their robes"* is a reference to arrogant ones. Some illustrations in the books on Roman and Greek history depict people whose skirts trail along the ground; this was part of a show of ostentation and arrogance. In fact, this is even more apparent in the films made in connection with this period. The actual topic here, the point being made by the Prophet, is not people lowering or dragging their garments, but the fact that they do this as a demonstration of arrogance.

There are many verses of the Qur'an and hadith that mention the negative consequences of pride and arrogance. In another hadith the Prophet stated that *"Anyone who has in their hearts a grain of pride will not enter Paradise"* (Muslim, Tirmidhi, Abu Dawud). God closes off the path of faith to those who have a trace of pride or arrogance in their hearts. This is revealed in the Qur'an as follows:

> *I will turn away from My Revelations and signs those who act with haughtiness on earth against all right. And though they see every sign (of the truth), they do not believe in it; and though they see the way of right guidance, they do not take it as a way to follow. But if they see the way of error and rebellion against the truth, they take it as a way to follow. That is because they deny Our Revelations and are ever heedless of them.* (Araf 7:146)

Pride is a screen which blinds the human soul; a person overwhelmed with pride will never perceive or understand the significance of the wonders of the earth and creation. When heedlessness befalls humanity they lose all sense of perception. Supremacy is an attribute reserved for the Supreme One only; how could this truth, which is declared five times every day from the mosques all over the world, be attributed to any other being?

In a hadith qudsi God Almighty declares: *"Pride is My cloak and greatness is My robe, and I shall cast into Hellfire he who competes with Me in respect of either"* (Abu Dawud, Muslim, Ibn Maja).

Pride, greatness and supremacy are all attributes of the Creator. However, while the condition of the human souls and human attributes are indeterminate, pride and greatness are a declaration of God's existence;

whoever attempts to share these attributes will be subjected to the flames of Hell.

A soul that is spurred on by pride cannot be blessed by faith; in other words faith will not enter a heart that favors anything except above and besides God. This is the state of a human who represents arrogance with their behavior and actions and this state is described by the Prophet as: *"those who trail their robes."*

The second of those deserving this harsh punishment are the *mannan*, who put others under obligation by mentioning the favor they made to them. The word *mannan* denotes miserliness as well. God gives them prosperity, so that they benefit from this blessing and let others benefit by giving in charity, and in return God will reward them generously. However, these people do not support the needy, and when they do, they nullify their good deed by mentioning their help to put people under an obligation, forgetting that both humans and their wealth belong to the Creator. A person with wealth has only one duty, and that is to provide to others with the wealth that has been bestowed upon them for the pleasure of God. However, some people's sole ambition in generosity is to obtain the gratitude of others for the wealth that was not theirs in the first place. Such an attitude is a total display of heedlessness, which results in a terrible downfall.

While God provides some humans with prosperity, He gives others a right over the wealth of those who are more fortunate. There are always some who are miserly and when they give in charity they remind the poor of this so-called good deed and generosity of theirs. Turning down people politely is better than abusing such a deed.

Another characteristic of those who abuse their deeds, the *mannan*, is miserliness. Miserliness distances a person from their Creator, from Paradise and from other humans, while at the same time leads them to the gates of Hell. We can understand this from a hadith: *"The miserly man is removed from God, from Paradise, from other men and is near Hell"* (Tirmidhi, Birr, 40).

The phrases in the hadith are used respectively. *"God will not look at them"* corresponds to the *mannan*, who pays no heed to others nor to supports them. They will be treated in the same way. God will show no compassion towards those who never showed compassion in this world to oth-

82

ers, to those who ignored the needs of other human beings nor to those who nullified their good deeds by boasting about the charity given. Such people will face a punishment in the Hereafter that is equal to that which they did to others here on earth.

The arrogant and conceited ones who trail their robes, strut around, and condescend when they speak to others out of haughtiness must realize that they too will face the same fate. The Creator will ignore them and not speak to them in the Hereafter. Such people should be aware that there are grave consequences and thus avoid this path that leads to eternal punishment.

Making false promises or taking oaths is an unadvisable act; however, some people deceive others by making false oaths solely for worldly benefits, lying and deceiving others to sell their goods at a profit. This is the third path that leads humans to the darkness of destruction; in the hadith such people are warned with the words *"God will not redeem them."*

Therefore, the third category of people who are doomed with the same punishment are those who deceive others with false statements regarding their goods, that is, those who believe they can deceive others with lies and deception.

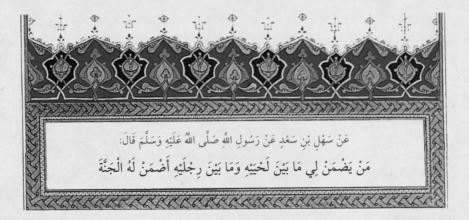

عَنْ سَهْلِ بْنِ سَعْدٍ عَنْ رَسُولِ اللَّهِ صَلَّى اللَّهُ عَلَيْهِ وَسَلَّمَ قَالَ:

مَنْ يَضْمَنْ لِي مَا بَيْنَ لَحْيَيْهِ وَمَا بَيْنَ رِجْلَيْهِ أَضْمَنْ لَهُ الْجَنَّةَ

BEING CAREFUL OF ONE'S TONGUE
AND CHASTITY

"Whoever guarantees for me what is between his jaws and
what is between his legs, I guarantee for him Paradise."

(Bukhari, Riqaq, 23; Tirmidhi, Zuhd, 61)

These words, a declaration by Prophet Muhammad, are a promise made by a man who was aware of what promises he was able to make. If the Prophet guaranteed the gardens of Paradise it is certain that this will be the reward for such people. The Prophet loved Uthman ibn Madun like a brother. When this Companion passed away, his wife said: *"May God be merciful to you. Now you have gone to Paradise."* The *Prophet objected and said: "Although I am God's Messenger, I do not know what will be done to him."* (Bukhari, Janaiz, 3)

This was a guarantee based on what God taught His Messenger. Therefore, if human beings can control their speech and guard their chastity in this world, they are sure to be protected against the flames of Hell. The Prophet of God has given us a promise of Paradise and there is no doubt that he will come to our aid and intercede for us on the Day of Judgment.

The tongue is an organ of huge importance, blessed with the ability of speech. However, when people use the tongue to speak in a bad way it becomes an organ of evil that can lead humans to disaster and destruction. The tongue should be an organ used to praise and express thanks to the Creator, to recite the Qur'an, the book of the universe, and to spread the command and words of the Qur'an and the hadith to others. With the tongue a non-Muslim can accept the faith and bear witness to the fact that God is one.

However, the tongue can also lead humans to destruction and grief; it can be the means of blasphemy and ingratitude, while the greatest evil and most unforgivable sin of reviling the Creator and His Messenger is done by means of speech. Lying, gossip and slander are all sins committed with the tongue and these evil words lead humans to perdition.

The Prophet tells us *"speak within the legitimate boundaries and I guarantee you Paradise."* Here we are not being told not to speak, but rather to avoid harmful speech, to use our tongues for beneficial deeds and in the proper manner.

Our genitals, or as referred to the Prophet, that which lies between our two legs, carry great significance for humanity. They were the reason for the expulsion of Adam from the gardens of Paradise. Although our genitals are the means for the continuation of mankind, leading to new generations, they can also lead to adultery and prostitution, the path of destruction for many societies; this kind of abuse leads to loss of family lines and the most fundamental legal rights.

When a child is illegitimate many problems arise. Who is the father of the child? What are the rights of inheritance? How do we protect the family system? And as a direct consequence of the disintegration of the family, how can we prevent the destruction of society? The answer to all these questions is deeply connected with the decency and chastity of a nation, that is, with humans guarding that which lies between their legs. While people of chastity and their descendents maintain their decency within the family and society until the Day of Judgment, the nations and individuals who pursue lives of adultery and prostitution will never progress to be a nation of prosperity.

Fundamentally, just as with any other subject, the boundaries drawn by religion are wide enough to find satisfaction leaving no need for a person to participate in illegitimate relations. It is for this reason that Prophet Muhammad said: *"Get married and reproduce, for I will take pride (in your numbers) on the Day of Judgment"* (Bukhari, Janaiz, 3). The Prophet will take pride in the great numbers of his community and his follow-

85

ers in comparison to other communities on the Day of Judgment, for the community of Muslims will be so vast in number that they will greatly outshine from others. The increase of believers is also related to keeping chaste and having children in the legitimate way. This critical issue determines whether the offspring will be legitimate or illegitimate.

Intimacy with one's lawful spouse merits a spiritual reward as a *wajib* act. When the Companions learned this from the Prophet, they were greatly surprised. When they asked him more about the subject, he smiled and replied with a question whether it is not sinful if not done in the lawful manner (Muslim, Zakat, 53). What is incumbent on Muslims is to avoid illegitimate paths and therefore choosing the legitimate path naturally is meritorious.

We should always consider that although this is a subject that may be embarrassing for some, it is an aspect of human nature, experienced even by the Prophets. If such an emotion, such a need, had not been given to Adam, then how would Prophet Muhammad, the most honorable person in the universe, have come into existence?

It is important to focus on a very important point here, the Prophet promises Paradise for those who can guarantee that what lies between their jaws and their legs has been kept away from sin; this means that there are people who can obtain the same reward due to their devotion and spiritual progress. Here, the subject of honor and merit is administered as a reward for guarding that which lies between the jaws and the legs. This is because to control these two organs means that one is controlling the desires of the soul for the sake of God, and especially at a time when a person is the most vulnerable and exposed to all kinds of evil.

This is a time when one's ego overtakes their soul and willpower; control at such a moment is extremely important, for it can be the means of attaining a great spiritual level, not to mention promise of Paradise. Those who resist the rampant desires of their souls when they are most vulnerable, those who seek refuge in Divine existence and refrain from evil and sin, in particular, those who continuously take every precaution possible to prevent themselves from encountering such a situation, may suddenly make great spiritual progress. Such progress could possibly take years of vigils and fasting. We should not undermine supererogatory worship anyway; but one needs to realize the importance of self-control mentioned in the hadith in relation to human perfection.

عَنْ أَبِي هُرَيْرَةَ أَنَّ رَسُولَ اللَّهِ صَلَّى اللَّهُ عَلَيْهِ وَسَلَّمَ قَالَ:
أَلَا أَدُلُّكُمْ عَلَى مَا يَمْحُو اللَّهُ بِهِ الْخَطَايَا وَيَرْفَعُ بِهِ الدَّرَجَاتِ قَالُوا بَلَى يَا
رَسُولَ اللَّهِ قَالَ إِسْبَاغُ الْوُضُوءِ عَلَى الْمَكَارِهِ وَكَثْرَةُ الْخُطَا إِلَى الْمَسَاجِدِ
وَانْتِظَارُ الصَّلَاةِ بَعْدَ الصَّلَاةِ فَذَلِكُمُ الرِّبَاطُ فَذَلِكُمُ الرِّبَاطُ فَذَلِكُمُ الرِّبَاطُ

(26)

ACTIONS WHICH ELIMINATE SIN AND
EXALT THE RANK OF BELIEVERS

"Shall I not guide you to that by which God erases faults and elevates
spiritual ranks?" They (the hearers) said: "Yes, Messenger of God." He
said: "Performing the ablution thoroughly despite difficulties, walking
much to the mosque, and waiting for the next prayer after observing a
prayer; this is devotion (to God, like a loyal border sentinel)."

(Muslim, Tahara, 41)

This hadith begins with the phrase *"A-la"* (*Shall I not?*) which is used in Arabic to warn the audience to pay attention before saying something important; the matters to be stated in the hadith require taking heed. There are certain matters which are possible to be mindful of even whilst asleep; matters such as avoiding backbiting or other sins. Nevertheless, realizing the acts mentioned in the hadith requires watchfulness.

One of the words in the hadith that attracts our attention is the word *"khata"* (mistake, fault, sin). Every one of us commits faults. We can even say that one who claims to be free of faults commits the greatest fault; the only exceptions are the Prophets. As Prophet Muhammad said: *"Every person sins. And the best of those who sin are those who repent"* (Muslim, Tahara, 41). Thus, he gives us the key in order to avoid and be misled towards evil.

Merely avoiding or escaping sin is not enough for a Muslim; one must work to achieve a higher rank. The elimination of sins leads us to this point to an extent, and the implementation of other good deeds and actions enables a human being to reach exceptional heights of faith. Therefore, it is by virtue of both negative and positive actions that individuals can elevate themselves, heading towards infinity and the ocean of divine attainment.

The first of these actions is making ablutions under the most difficult conditions, for example, in the cold of winter, when the water is very cold. Whatever the conditions, the ablutions must be made as perfectly as possible.

The second action is to attend mosques for prayers; a life spent on the path towards the places of worship is a life that resembles the seed of prosperity. The seed spends years growing in the earth and flourishes to produce the fruits of Paradise in the Hereafter. This attendance mentioned refers to going to the mosques no matter how far they are, and also encourages the continuance of such a habit.

The third action is to perform one prayer and then to willingly wait for the next prayer time to come, or as narrated in another hadith, *"attaching one's heart to the mosque"* (Muslim, Tahara, 41). Prayer is the relaxation of the soul and the refreshment of conscience. Everyone has a passion for something in life and Prophet Muhammad was no exception. The Messenger's overwhelming passion was for prayer and this is why he would always say *"Comfort us, O Bilal!"* (make the call to prayer). He also stated that prayer was the light of his eyes. (Majmu al-Jawaid).

In the hadith three different subjects are discussed, but when we examine these subjects more closely, we immediately notice that the three are all connected to prayer. Prayer is such an important aspect of our life; it is the means of ascendance for believers, awakening people to realities in the best possible form. Prayer is the pillar of religion, enforcing the emotions of faith into the soul. Without prayer, faith weakens. As prayer is directly related to guidance, it needs to be observed in a becoming fashion. The duty of worship must be performed by focusing on the prayer and the soul must be free from any kind of worldly preoccupation. It is for this reason that it is not advisable for a person to perform the prayer while feeling the need to answer a call of nature. Such a feeling is both a distraction for the individual and a display of disrespect towards worship. Prayer is an act carried out for human enlightenment and not a simplistic duty to be hurried or performed in a distracted state.

The rituals performed while preparing for the prayer, those that ensure that we stand before our Creator in a composed state, are also actions that gain us merit. So before we begin praying we must first purify our hearts of everything that might distract us from our duty; we must stand before the Creator in prayer, totally focused with the emotion of worship in our souls. We will be rewarded for every step we take when ensuring the validity and stability of our prayer until we actually stand in submission before the Creator. Our sole intention in this preparation is to perform the prayer in a state of tranquility, for a believer's intention is better than their actions. If a non-Muslim were to carry out these actions they receive no reward, whereas a Muslim is rewarded even when relieving themselves, because there is a reward in eliminating impurities.

Performing ablutions properly play a significant role in the spiritual preparation for prayer; whether this is due to the body being stimulated when the limbs come into contact with water or due to some other reason, the result is invariably the same. Generally though, we don't seem to consider the actual wisdom of purification when carrying out the ablutions; whereas ablution is the reason to bring the focus that the first thing that comes to mind would be prayer.

In addition to the initial preparation and the ablution itself, *adhan* is another step toward prayer. As a matter of fact, fulfilling the *sunna* acts such as reciting the prayers for ablution helps deepen the metaphysical awareness; and after the completion of the initial *sunna* prayer, the believer is ready to observe the obligatory prayer. This, for the believers, is the last joyful step in fulfilling their duty. If at this point there is no feeling of excitement or pleasure in your soul and it is not possible to concentrate on the union with the Creator, then you should realize that there is some flaw in your actions.

When the muezzin makes the call to prayer, every aspect of human life that distracts a believer from God is diminished and the believer declares *Allahu Akbar*, "God is the greatest," beginning the prayer with complete concentration and repeating these words of glorification with every bow and prostration of worship, declaring the greatness of the Creator while expressing their own insignificance. It is in this way that they are able to reach a state of total submission and a true awareness of servitude and adoration. This is a general account of a prayer in full concentration. The greetings of a person of sincerity, a true believer, reach the Creator during their prayer. In the same way, Prophet Muhammad bestowed greetings on the Creator on the night of ascension and God bestowed His greetings in return.

The phrase *mahw* used in the hadith means erasing something written. So we can infer that a potential for fault is ingrained in our nature. While some people let this seed flourish, others prevent it from growing. If humans were to abide by the advice of Prophet Muhammad, God the Merciful would eliminate these sins or mistakes and turn the aptitude of evil into the aptitude of excellence, as indicated in the following verse from the Qur'an: *God effaces what He wills (of things and events He has created, and laws He has established), and He confirms and establishes (what He wills): with Him is the Mother of the Book.* (Ra'd 13:39). Thus, if the ability to err is an inevitable aspect of human nature, eliminating the error or "erasing faults" is surely something that of common concern to all mankind.

Every human being is exposed to sin and some live lives of total depravation, but we should all be aware that it is always possible to eliminate these sins and errors and replace them with sublime actions. One of the paths that leads to such prosperity is to first perform the ablution, regardless of any difficulty, and secondly to make a habit of regularly attending mosques. One should leave the mosque with the sincere intention of attending the next prayer. One should feel as if their soul has remained in this sacred place of spiritual bliss; thus one is returning to be reunited with one's soul. The third path is to wait for the next prayer after having prayed with complete devotion. All of these are actions that eliminate sins and exalt a person, rank by rank towards the highest level of their personal capacity.

In the Arabic text of the hadith the Prophet refers to these actions as *ribat* repeating this word three times. *Ribat* literally means to stand sentinel at the borders of one's homeland. *Ribat* in this context not only refers to a flow of spiritual and material prosperity, but this word also indicates watchfulness against matters that can lead to every kind of sin. It implies devotion and commitment, like a soldier who devotes himself to guarding against danger.

In Qur'an we are ordered:

> *O you who believe! Be patient (persevere through what befalls you in the world in God's cause); encourage each other to patience vying in it with one another and outdoing all others in it; and observe your duties to God in solidarity, and keep from disobedience to God in due reverence for Him and piety, so that you may prosper (in both worlds)*. (Al-Imran 3:200)

The imperative form of *ribat* (i.e. *rabitu*) in this verse can be translated as *"observe your duties to God in solidarity."* So a person who makes ablutions and constantly attends the mosque, or has the intention of attending, or whose soul is emotionally attached to places of worship at all times is a person who tries to observe his duties and is truly devoted to God.

With this hadith the Prophet is actually telling us that, the term *ribat* is normally used for the duty of border sentinels. As such a sentinel is watchful against enemy attacks; we also need to be watchful of our struggle against the two enemies, the Devil and our carnal self. In a way, this latter duty requires greater effort. We are responsible for both types of struggle—the lesser jihad and the greater jihad respectively. While defending his homeland, a man does not have much time to think about the passing fancies of this world and such a person is less likely to be overpowered by his carnal desires since he is preoccupied with his struggle. However, when he begins to lead an easy life, he is prone to be taken over by temptations. A person is responsible for protecting his or her soul against dangers and resisting evil. This is the greater form of *jihad*. The most effective weapon in this kind of *jihad* is prayer. *Jihad* is in some cases obligatory on all Muslims, while in other situations it is a communal obligation and there is joint obligation for the material *jihad* and the *jihad* of the soul. This is why Prophet Muhammad said while returning from a battle: *"We have returned from the lesser jihad to the greater jihad."*

Thus, to briefly summarize our observations regarding this hadith we can see that two of these topics are mainly action oriented, while the third refers to intention. These are three subjects that totally encapsulate human emotions and concepts. According to the Qur'anic principle, *good deeds wipe out evil deeds* (Hud 11:114), believers are purified of their past sins by virtue of realizing these three things, which equip them with a passion for worship, devotion to the Almighty, and sincere intention in order to fight against the possible faults in the future.

In the first instance a person must have a passion for servitude and a great desire to obtain the divine reward to be able to endure the difficulties of performing the ablutions at times of hardship, for example, when the water is too cold or when it is so scarce that every last drop is a blessing. Therefore, when a human can perform the ablutions regardless of the hardships they face, this is an expression of their profound dedication. It is then that the soul is truly in a state of total devotion; nevertheless, the shared aspect of the points we have discussed here is devotion.

The second aspect is that—leaving aside the physical benefits of walking to mosques—regular attendance to places of worship means stepping into a virtuous cycle where an act of goodness paves the way for another: the soul reaches a state of elation that exceeds human comprehension; even before entering the prayer, the heart is absorbed in a state of spirituality; one is prepared to stand before the Creator in submission with total concentration, which is an important aspect of worship; walking towards worship provides an opportunity for contemplation, which leads to self-supervision and repentance… A person who resolved to journey within this cycle is a candidate for forgiveness as stated in the verse: …*That God may forgive you your lapses of the past and those to follow* (Fath 48:2).

The third aspect is looking forward to the next prayer as if waiting for the beloved, using the times of worship and divine prosperity as though they were a part of our daily schedule and planning our daily routine around the times of prayer. Such an understanding of time totally exceeds the human imagination; it is only an intention of such magnitude, that is, the intention of worship, which can possibly complete and complement the emptiness that remains in a person's daily life. It is only then that it is possible to convey the emotions of the prayer, the feeling of tranquility, all the sense of affiliation with the Creator into the daily activities. This constant connection between God and worldly affairs will transform these routine actions into forms of worship. Add to this the sincerity of human intention and this will be the means of transforming that which limits us into an infinite ocean of virtue. Therefore, the prayer must be performed with a soul full of emotion and aspiration, like a *jihad* of materiality and spirituality; this is the designation for a believer.

عَنْ أَبِي هُرَيْرَةَ رَضِيَ اللهُ عَنْهُ عَنِ النَّبِيِّ صَلَّى اللهُ عَلَيْهِ وَسَلَّمَ قَالَ:

قَالَ اللهُ أَعْدَدْتُ لِعِبَادِي الصَّالِحِينَ مَا لَا عَيْنٌ رَأَتْ وَلَا أُذُنٌ سَمِعَتْ

وَلَا خَطَرَ عَلَى قَلْبِ بَشَرٍ

(27)

THE SURPRISES AWAITING THE
RIGHTEOUS SERVANT

*"God the most exalted said: I have prepared for My righteous
servants what no eye has seen and what no ear has heard,
nor has it occurred to the human heart"*

(Bukhari, Tawhid, 35; Muslim, Janna, 4)

This hadith refers to a surprise for believers, speaking of the most unexpected things arriving at the most unexpected times. Although Qur'an mentions some of the blessings that await the faithful ones, humans will be unable to understand the reality and true value of the existence of these until they attain them.

In his interpretation of a verse (Baqara 2:25) of the Qur'an, concerning the fruits of Paradise, Ibn Abbas states that these things are fruits that human beings have not experienced before but that when we taste them we will be reminded of something that we have eaten in the past. These are not the same fruit that we have here, for the fruit of Paradise has been created in conformity with the eternity and immortality of Paradise itself. Thus, seeking the fruit of this world in Paradise would be nothing less than simple mindedness.

Paradise is a place of surprises; another one of the surprises of Paradise is reunion with the Creator, for the thousands of years of life in Paradise. This bliss beyond imagination awaits the sincere believers of servitude.

The *salih* (righteous) ones mentioned in the hadith are those who fully perform actions free from flaws while *salihat* (good deeds) are the actual actions that are performed to perfection. The only way to understand if actions are flawless is to compare them with the divine criteria; that is, how is the prayer performed according to the divine commands, how do we fast and give in charity, how do we struggle in the way of God, how do we control our ego, how do we elevate the soul, how do we strengthen our willpower and how do we develop our emotions and feelings? All these questions are subjected and assessed according to divine regulations; therefore, in the first stage towards perfection, a human being must calculate and regulate their actions according to the divine declarations so that they will give pleasure and delight to their Creator. Like the musician who takes great care in tuning his instrument to please the audience we must prepare ourselves prior to standing before the Creator according to the commands of the Qur'an so that we will be among those who are favored by God.

Another explanation of *salihat* (good deeds) is that, these actions should be done to the best of our ability, with the awareness of seeking divine approval. As believers we must make every effort to fulfill the duties that have been bestowed upon us, since which exact actions of ours will be the means to our salvation cannot be defined or known. This is the reason Prophet Muhammad, peace and blessings be upon him, said: *"Fear God and never disparage (underestimate) a good deed"* (Abu Dawud, Libas, 25).

In addition, the Merciful One speaks of: *"My righteous servants"* in the hadith. Righteousness brings people closer to God and they become His beloved servants. God's affection for His servants is expressed in another hadith: *"When I love (a servant) I am his ears with which he hears, his eyes which he sees, his hand with which he strikes and his foot with which he walks"* (Bukhari, Riqaq, 38).

Therefore, a servant who continuously performs good deeds comes so close to their Creator that their every action is under divine guidance; can you imagine, a devoted believer is guided towards the path of truth with every step they take? Such a person can only be one who turns to their Creator, towards divine beneficence. Such a person has reached the status of *"My righteous servant,"* and is accepted as one who has reached divine affiliation. Such a person constantly pleas with their Lord: *"O God! Hold me and guide me for I am nothing without You!"*

Giving water to a thirsty dog can sometimes be the means of entering Paradise, while depriving a cat of food can lead to Hellfire. (Bukhari, Anbiya, 54). Attaining Paradise and the rewards given in Paradise is a total surprise, a divine mystery. We can only recognize the things we actually see or hear in this world. Actually, our imagination is also limited by the capacity of our senses here. Therefore, it is not possible for us to fathom the blessings in an infinite realm.

Another aspect could be that the Creator rewards our good deeds sometimes ten, a hundred, or seven hundred times over or more but it is impossible for a believer to know the reward that awaits them. Thus, when we are awarded for our deeds in the Hereafter we will be amazed, as the merits bestowed upon us are beyond our imagination.

عَنْ أَبِي هُرَيْرَةَ أَنَّ رَسُولَ اللهِ صَلَّى اللهُ عَلَيْهِ وَسَلَّمَ قَالَ:

حُجِبَتِ النَّارُ بِالشَّهَوَاتِ وَحُجِبَتِ الْجَنَّةُ بِالْمَكَارِهِ

28

PARADISE IS SURROUNDED BY HARDSHIP
AND HELL IS SURROUNDED BY DESIRES

"Hell is surrounded by lusts and Paradise is surrounded by things displeasing to the carnal self."

(Bukhari, Riqaq, 28; Muslim, Janna, 1)

Hell is screened by lusts, whereas Paradise is hidden by apparent hardships and undesirable aspects. For those who pursue everything for the material value, the difficulties on the path that leads to Paradise may not seem to be very appealing. Primarily, both Paradise and Hell are a blessing for human beings, for one is a form of encouragement for those seeking the true path, while the other is terrifying, a path of fear. When a human sees the incentives that lie on the path of benefaction they struggle to reach Paradise, and when they see the dreadful path that leads to Hell they make every effort to avoid its evil, turning back to the path of righteousness; in this way both paths become a form of mercy for us.

The Almighty One has put Paradise and Hell in different coverings. Then He presented them to human beings as exchanges for their deeds; we make a choice between the paths leading to either destination by using our free will. Paradise is a precious pearl screened by an unattractive shell; performing the rituals of purification and prayer, the pilgrimage, giving to charity, striving to remove the obstacles between people and God and, bearing difficulties and mistreatment for His sake are among the elements of this shell. Those who only see the outward face are always misguided. Therefore, the candidates for Hell outnumber those of Paradise.

Humans tend to choose the easier alternative; those who think "Prayer is beneficial, but praying five times every day is too difficult" avoid this duty, which is of great benefit, out of their petty calculations. The difficulty of performing the ritual of purification under harsh winter conditions is one of the main reasons why people abandon the duties bestowed upon them. However, we are told in the hadith that those who endure hardships will be able to move one step closer to the gates of Paradise; this is also pertinent to fasting, giving charity, performing the hajj and other duties.

Various trivial things that prevent an intelligent person from acting with a sense of consciousness are also forms of deceit that prevent one from entering the gardens of Paradise; the fire of Hell is a place of destruction which lures us with ambition and desire. Most of those who choose the path of evil are unaware of the agonizing trap they are about to fall into, like a fly landing on poisoned honey. Passion is nothing but a poison; it destroys those who dare to reach to it like fire destroys the moths that approach the heat of the flames. With total ignorance, people approach passion that screens evil and suddenly find themselves in the burning flames of Hell. Before they have the chance to escape this trap, they are lured on by attractions that pull them ever deeper into the burning flames.

The apparent burdens around the path to Paradise do not deceive those who know the Prophet, one who stands on the crossroads of the two paths. Such people will find guidance to the path of truth from his words of wisdom. They will find the way that leads to the gates of Paradise, for their souls have embraced the desire to reach the prosperity of the garden. However, others who seek the pleasures of prosperity elsewhere live steeped in the deceit of passion and the artificial blessings of their so-called heaven in this world. But the fact of the matter is that those who live in this heaven of materialism will never reach the true prosperity that awaits the devoted believer in Paradise, not even for a moment.

Faith and blasphemy are like seeds which will reveal their true faces in the next world and transform into Paradise and Hell; this means that despite what might seem to be difficult, a believer actually lives the life of Paradise in the world of mortality. The truth of the matter is that it is inconceivable for a person who is aware of the benefits of Paradise to reject the chance of eternal happiness and take the path to Hell; what deceives people are the cloaks they wear. If we re-examine the words of Prophet we can see how significant they are; here laid out before us the consequences of following the two paths—the prosperous path which leads to happiness and contentment and the path which leads to fear and destruction.

عَنِ الْعِرْبَاضِ بْنِ سَارِيَةَ قَالَ:

وَعَظَنَا رَسُولُ اللهِ صَلَّى اللهُ عَلَيْهِ وَسَلَّمَ يَوْمًا بَعْدَ صَلَاةِ الْغَدَاةِ مَوْعِظَةً بَلِيغَةً

ذَرَفَتْ مِنْهَا الْعُيُونُ وَوَجِلَتْ مِنْهَا الْقُلُوبُ فَقَالَ رَجُلٌ إِنَّ هَذِهِ مَوْعِظَةُ مُوَدِّع

فَمَاذَا تَعْهَدُ إِلَيْنَا يَا رَسُولَ اللهِ قَالَ أُوصِيكُمْ بِتَقْوَى اللهِ وَالسَّمْعِ وَالطَّاعَةِ

وَإِنْ عَبْدٌ حَبَشِيٌّ فَإِنَّهُ مَنْ يَعِشْ مِنْكُمْ يَرَى اخْتِلَافًا كَثِيرًا

وَإِيَّاكُمْ وَمُحْدَثَاتِ الْأُمُورِ فَإِنَّهَا ضَلَالَةٌ فَمَنْ أَدْرَكَ ذَلِكَ مِنْكُمْ

فَعَلَيْهِ بِسُنَّتِي وَسُنَّةِ الْخُلَفَاءِ الرَّاشِدِينَ الْمَهْدِيِّينَ عَضُّوا عَلَيْهَا بِالنَّوَاجِذِ

(29)

THREE OBLIGATIONS: GOD, THE STATE AND FAITH

"The Messenger of God prayed with us. After the prayer he turned towards us and delivered an impressive sermon which made us weep and our hearts tremble. A person said: O Messenger of God, today you have delivered a sermon as if it was your last one. What do you advise us? The Messenger of God said: "I advise you to fear God and obey your leader, even if he is a black slave. Those of you who live long enough will see great controversy. Beware of newly invented matters in religion, for every invented matter is going astray, and every going astray is in Hellfire; so cling to my Sunna and the Sunna of the rightly guided caliphs (as if you were clenching it between your teeth)."

(Abu Dawud, Sunna, 5; Tirmidhi, Ilm, 16)

In this hadith, Prophet Muhammad mentions three obligations. The first is piety or *taqwa*; this is our obligation towards the Creator. The second is listening to and obeying a leader, which is our obligation to the state, while the third is following the traditions of the Prophet. This last obligation is our duty to religion.

The word *taqwa* (piety, God consciousness) comes from the root *wiqaya* (protection). In a sense, it means coming under the protection of God by acting in accordance with the laws of creation. It is an obligation for Muslims to listen and obey the commands of the person they choose as the leader, no matter who they are. This is a form of democracy that is superior to all others, and is one that was brought into force fourteen centuries ago.

People today have been unsuccessful in maintaining such a form of democracy; indeed, they will never be able to attain it if the world continues to advance in the way it has been. However, it would be wrong to refer to a system that was introduced by Prophet Muhammad as a democratic system; nowhere else in the world has such a system been established. In some nations, people of different races or religions are still viewed as being inferior, whereas Islam commands obedience to anyone if they have been brought to power according to the will of society. Caliphate was open to all and society would chose any leader they wished; once the leader was in power the community was then obliged to obey the caliph. In fact, what is important here is not the person who is the leader, but the fact that the leader has been selected by the society.

In Qur'an God states that the religion has been completed: *This day I have perfected your religion…* (Al-Maida 5:3). There was nothing left to be said and no place for any thing innovated to be introduced into the religion. Anything new that was introduced into the religion would result in one or more of the Prophet's traditions being nullified. It is for this reason that embracing the traditions of the Prophet and the caliphs who were under his guidance is a necessity for all Muslims. The traditions of the Prophet are a great blessing to mankind, and they must be learned and protected, for these traditions should be taught to forthcoming generations so they can be protected.

عَنْ أَبِي هُرَيْرَةَ قَالَ قَالَ رَسُولُ اللهِ صَلَّى اللهُ عَلَيْهِ وَسَلَّمَ:

اَلنَّاسُ مَعَادِنُ كَمَعَادِنِ الْفِضَّةِ وَالذَّهَبِ خِيَارُهُمْ فِي الْجَاهِلِيَّةِ خِيَارُهُمْ فِي الْإِسْلَامِ

إِذَا فَقُهُوا وَالْأَرْوَاحُ جُنُودٌ مُجَنَّدَةٌ فَمَا تَعَارَفَ مِنْهَا اثْتَلَفَ وَمَا تَنَاكَرَ مِنْهَا اخْتَلَفَ

(30)

PEOPLE ARE LIKE MINES

"People resemble raw metals like gold and silver; the best ones in the Jahiliya (Days of Ignorance) if they enter Islam and assimilate in it are the best. Souls are like troops of soldiers. The souls that recognize one another come together and those that do not recognize one another are remote from one another."

(Bukhari, Anbiya, 2; Muslim, Birr, 159)

It is as if Prophet Muhammad had gathered all the pedagogues and psychologists together and was lecturing them. When educating people it is very important to recognize their characteristics first. Quite often, physical features reveal much about the inner worlds of people.

Education with no form of knowledge or training is doomed to be ineffective, and in some situations can even be harmful. This is why God revealed: *Say (to them, O Messenger): "This is my way: I call to God on clear evidence and with sure knowledge—I and those who follow me."* (Yusuf 12:108)

As we see from this verse, the invitation to a mission or way of thought must be made with awareness and knowledge. An action performed with insight is an action that is undertaken with the knowledge of the method of how to approach and invite people to a cause with total consciousness of the nature and limits of the invitation. Some humans have the capability of understanding and finding the spiritual essence with minimal encouragement, while others need words of advice and wisdom given to them on a regular basis. Still others require greater attention and perceptivity. However, the only way to discover the potentialities of the individual is through discretion and precaution.

Those who were the most conscious, perceptive, righteous and just during the Era of Ignorance were among the most excellent followers after they learned the truth and beauty of Islam. If a precious metal like gold or silver is melted to a certain consistency it does not transform into another substance, but rather remains gold or silver. This is the reason why the Companions and sincere followers were compared to precious metals. Those with souls of gold during the Era of Ignorance were the same with the advent of Islam, but only when they accepted Islam and strengthened their knowledge and faith.

Of course, for the believers to reach such a consistency they needed a great teacher, a guide of extraordinary talent and knowledge, for this was the only way they could absorb the beauty of Islam into their souls and reach the piety of faith.

عَنْ أَبِي مُوسَى رَضِيَ اللهُ عَنْهُ قَالَ قَالَ رَسُولُ اللهِ صَلَّى اللهُ عَلَيْهِ وَسَلَّمَ:

إِنَّ اللهَ لَيُمْلِي لِلظَّالِمِ حَتَّى إِذَا أَخَذَهُ لَمْ يُفْلِتْهُ قَالَ ثُمَّ قَرَأَ (وَكَذَلِكَ أَخْذُ رَبِّكَ

إِذَا أَخَذَ الْقُرَى وَهِيَ ظَالِمَةٌ إِنَّ أَخْذَهُ أَلِيمٌ شَدِيدٌ)

31

OPPRESSION WILL NOT GO UNPUNISHED

"Surely God grants the wrongdoer, the oppressor, a reprieve. But once He seizes him, He does not let him be saved." Then the Prophet recited: "Such is the chastisement of your Lord when He chastises communities in the midst of their wrong: grievous, indeed, and severe is His chastisement (11:102)."

(Bukhari, Tafsir al-Sura (11); Muslim, Birr, 61)

God gives the wrongdoers some time to repent and amend their behavior. If they do not take advantage of this opportunity, their persistence in wrongdoing becomes the last straw and the divine retribution follows.

There are a number of laws that are prescribed by the Creator that necessitates no reason for any variation. This is portrayed in this verse of the Qur'an: *No change can there be in God's creation.*" (Rum 30:30). One of these laws is that the tyrant is the weapon of God. The Prophet explained that the oppressor is the justice of God. He first uses the oppressor to retaliate against others and then takes revenge on the oppressor. (Ajluni, Kashf al-Khafa, 2:49).

The oppressors of the present day who continue with arrogance and no consideration for others; may have been granted a respite, this is only an interval given to them by God, for one day they in the Supreme Tribunal justice will be delivered.

There are many examples in the past of those who personally witnessed the Divine punishment and its consequences in their life times, for instance in the cases Sodom, Gomorra and Pompeii. There are many more examples that have been forgotten with the years. Similar examples can also be given from near history.

عَنْ أَبِي هُرَيْرَةَ عَنِ النَّبِيِّ صَلَّى اللهُ عَلَيْهِ وَسَلَّمَ قَالَ:

سَبْعَةٌ يُظِلُّهُمْ اللهُ فِي ظِلِّهِ يَوْمَ لَا ظِلَّ إِلَّا ظِلُّهُ الْإِمَامُ الْعَادِلُ

وَشَابٌّ نَشَأَ فِي عِبَادَةِ رَبِّهِ وَرَجُلٌ قَلْبُهُ مُعَلَّقٌ فِي الْمَسَاجِدِ

وَرَجُلَانِ تَحَابَّا فِي اللهِ اجْتَمَعَا عَلَيْهِ وَتَفَرَّقَا عَلَيْهِ وَرَجُلٌ طَلَبَتْهُ امْرَأَةٌ ذَاتُ

مَنْصِبٍ وَجَمَالٍ فَقَالَ إِنِّي أَخَافُ اللهَ وَرَجُلٌ تَصَدَّقَ أَخْفَى حَتَّى لَا تَعْلَمَ

شِمَالُهُ مَا تُنْفِقُ يَمِينُهُ وَرَجُلٌ ذَكَرَ اللهَ خَالِيًا فَفَاضَتْ عَيْنَاهُ

(32)

THE SEVEN GROUPS THAT WILL BE
PROTECTED BY THE DIVINE SHADE

*"God will shade seven (groups of) people under His shade on the
Day when there will be no shade except His: the just ruler; young
people who grew up in worship of God; a person whose heart is
attached to mosques; two persons who liked one another for God's
sake, who came together and departed on this basis; a man who
was called upon (to sin) by a woman of high status and beauty and*

turned down her offer, saying that he fears God; A person who gave
charity in such secrecy that even his left hand did not know what
his right hand had given; and a person whose eyes filled with tears
on mentioning God in solitude."

(Bukhari, Adhan, 36; Muslim, Zakat, 91)

Many of the topics mentioned in the above hadith may appear to be difficult to perform and very demanding, but each carries great significance for human willpower. Some people may be able to escape one of the pitfalls facing them, yet be lured into another. The only possible way to escape or avoid these disastrous and sometimes fatal pitfalls is to seek refuge in the mercy of the Creator and to embrace the divine commands of His eternal power. Therefore, human salvation, which lies in the strength of self-control, depends on a person's devotion and their bond with the Creator.

The above hadith is an offering to those who have willpower; it is for those who possess a power of devotion and a connection with God. An opportunity to attain the greatly sought-after divine protection of the Hereafter is offered. The hope that one will be able to fulfill these tasks, which are demanding and require endurance, and as a result be able to obtain a great reward in the Hereafter, fills our souls with aspiration and desire.

On the Day of Judgment, when the burning sun scorches through, the shade provided by the clouds, gleaming like flames of fire, when the means of salvation have faded away and everything weighs against mankind, there will be no other shade provided but that created by God's grace and protection. On that day the important fact will not be that the shade is the shade of Heaven; the important factor will be a shift in the rules, the transformation of the skies into shade for those who have earned it. Nobody will be able to aid or assist others on this devastating day, and there will certainly be no protection or favoritism. Who could possibly protect others on a day of such intensity when everyone will hold their breaths in both fear and anticipation of their reward or punishment?

On such a day there is only one possible place to seek refuge and that will be with Divine mercy. The ones who will be granted the shade of benevolence are:

1 – Those who are aware of their responsibilities and duties in the universe, the leaders of communities and nations who represent integrity, who carry out their duties of entrustment with compliance, justification and righteousness.

2 – Young people, who, despite their corporeal passions and desires, devotes themselves to serving God at a time of disruption and disorder.

3 – The devoted worshipper, who, ignoring the material ambitions of the world, constantly attends the mosque and other places of worship with the desire to serve.

4 – Those who love one another for the sake of God, those who come together and depart from one another with the yearning for the Divine in their souls. These are the ones who are devoted to the mission of truth whose motivation is the approval and love of God.

5 – The heroes who live a life of purity and honor, who throughout their lives protect their chastity and virtue and have the resolution and power to resist temptation and reject evil out of their fear of God.

6 – Those who give of their wealth in charity as an indication of their fidelity and devotion to God, those who give in secret, far from the eyes or knowledge of others, for the sake of obtaining Divine pleasure in such a way that the left hand is unaware of that which the right hand has given.

7 – Those who shed tears at times of solitude from the intense emotion and affection in the soul, who constantly obtain their power and self-control from the Creator. These are the heroes who have both the soul and emotion to destroy the aspiration of fear and passion with their astounding determination. This hadith actually guides human beings towards becoming nations of excellence and demonstrates the principles necessary for sustaining these actions.

عَنْ جَابِرِ بْنِ عَبْدِ اللَّهِ عَنِ النَّبِيِّ صَلَّى اللَّهُ عَلَيْهِ وَسَلَّمَ قَالَ:

أُعْطِيتُ خَمْسًا لَمْ يُعْطَهُنَّ أَحَدٌ قَبْلِي نُصِرْتُ بِالرُّعْبِ مَسِيرَةَ شَهْرٍ وَجُعِلَتْ
لِيَ الْأَرْضُ مَسْجِدًا وَطَهُورًا فَأَيُّمَا رَجُلٍ مِنْ أُمَّتِي أَدْرَكَتْهُ الصَّلَاةُ فَلْيُصَلِّ
وَأُحِلَّتْ لِيَ الْمَغَانِمُ وَلَمْ تَحِلَّ لِأَحَدٍ قَبْلِي وَأُعْطِيتُ الشَّفَاعَةَ
وَكَانَ النَّبِيُّ يُبْعَثُ إِلَى قَوْمِهِ خَاصَّةً وَبُعِثْتُ إِلَى النَّاسِ عَامَّةً

(33)

A BELIEVER IS A RESPONSIBLE PERSON

*"Each of you is a shepherd and each of you is responsible for what
you tend. The leader is a shepherd and is responsible for what he
tends; a man is the shepherd of his family and is responsible for
what he tends; a woman is the shepherd in the house of her husband
and is responsible for what she tends; a servant is the shepherd
of his master's wealth and is responsible for it. Each of you is a
shepherd and each of you is responsible for what you tend."*

(Bukhari, Juma 11; Muslim, Imara, 20)

T he actual meaning of the word "*rai*" in the Arabic text of the hadith is one who watches or guards over something; a shepherd is called *rai* because he looks after the flock that has been entrusted to him to the best of his ability. He leads them to graze in the most secure and fertile fields. He is upset and feels helpless when the herd is attacked by wolves or exposed to any other form of harm or danger. In short, a shepherd is supposed to bear great responsibility.

There is a similar relationship between the ruler of a state and the ones over whom they rule. It is the duty of the ruler and their representatives, according to their rank, to watch over and take care of the welfare of those who are under their care, to share their joy, their sorrows and hardships. They are responsible for ensuring the happiness and ease of the people and relieving their burdens and difficulties.

The relationship between a couple and their family members are also that of gentle care, protection and providence. Not only is a husband responsible for the maintenance of the family, for their material needs such as clothing and for providing a suitable home in which they can live; he needs to also provide for their immaterial needs such as education, balanced discipline, and ensure affectionate relations exist between the family members. The relationship between a wife and husband is not merely confined to socially assigned roles that once married spouses will readily assume responsibility of. In other words, the wife plays as critical a role in the overall management of her household as the husband. The shared partnership of raising a family and building a home together in a loving and trusting manner is at the kernel of good leadership. A wife is as much responsible as her husband for the overall management of the household and for protecting their shared wealth and honor.

In olden times, a servant's duty was to protect his or her master's wealth and estate; children need to protect their family's wealth, honor, and dignity. These forms of *rai* are all related to guarding and keeping a watchful eye on something. Therefore, we could say that from a religious point of view, if there is no sense of responsibility then there is no *rai*. Every person has some kind of responsibility towards others, like a shepherd to his flock; in fact, even if there is no incentive for protecting or keeping a watch over something, this is still a duty, a responsibility. Every human being is responsible for looking after and protecting their own *nafs*, mind, senses, and every organ in the body; these are all a trust and a great blessing.

Islam affords everyone a particular level of responsibility and in a complete sense outlines the principles that follows such responsibility, be it a ruler or a mother, a father, or the role a servant plays. Every sector within a society in general and the smaller units have all been given a certain responsibility and principles to adhere to. Such level of organization and arrangement for the overall orderliness and harmony of all aspects of society, where no one was neglected, occurred in a period when true democracy did not exist anywhere else in the world.

The Prophet defined the boundaries of a state leader's responsibility. He also reminded both women and men of the significant duties they play and gave them both certain responsibilities. A father's duty is to his children and the child's duty and responsibility is to the father, and there are obligations bestowed on both.

Many of the human and civil rights and duties that were developed only recently in our times; the Prophet had already presented them as a solution centuries ago.

The responsibilities of a leader and the duties of those under his rule, the rights and duties of a mother and father, the rights and duties of a husband and wife are discussed today in books of morality, education, sociology and law; compare these to the rights and responsibilities declared centuries ago by the Prophet of Islam.

عَنْ أَبِي هُرَيْرَةَ قَالَ قَالَ النَّبِيُّ صَلَّى اللَّه عَلَيْهِ وَسَلَّمَ:
اَلْإِحْسَانُ أَنْ تَعْبُدَ اللَّهَ كَأَنَّكَ تَرَاهُ فَإِنْ لَمْ تَكُنْ تَرَاهُ فَإِنَّهُ يَرَاكَ

(34)

EXCELLENCE IS WORSHIPPING GOD
AS IF YOU SEE HIM

"Ihsan is to worship God as though you see Him; even though you cannot see Him, know then indeed that He sees you."

(Bukhari, Tafsir (31) 2; Muslim, Iman, 5)

The integration of faith with Islam is living Islam within the boundaries of *ihsan*. Ihsan is the state of perpetual awareness of the Divine, worshipping Him as if one could see Him, and even though one cannot see Him, know and be deeply aware that He sees one. This constant awareness and level of Divine consciousness is the peak of spiritual perfection that a believer can potentially reaches at. It is excellence and perfect goodness, and this is the distinguishing characteristic of the best of believers. A believer's reaching a transcendent dimension within faith and Islam and showing due performance is a type of *ihsan*. As stated in the Qur'an: "*…is the recompense of ihsan (in obedience to God) other than ihsan? (Rahman 55:60),*" the Almighty Creator generously rewards this sincere devotion with blessings which "*no eye has ever seen, no ear has ever heard, and never occurred to a human heart*" (Bukhari, Muslim).

Relatively speaking, the aspect that looks at the servant's level of *ihsan* is in the form of sincerity, noble behavior, respect and awe, whereas that aspect that looks to the Divine is the *ihsan* that manifests God's filling of His servants' hearts with faith and divine inspirations, removing the veils from their eyes and revealing the truth of materiality, protecting their mouths from unnecessary speech, inspiring them with utterances of words of wisdom, or awakening them to Divine manifestations. The believers who reach this point, where the realms beyond the visible existence begin to be unveiled, feel as if they were about to see Him. Together with being conscious of the fact "*No vision can grasp Him,*" they lose themselves with the idea of seeing Him and with the awe of being seen by Him. In a medley of obedience, sincerity, self-effacement, and awe, such people feel the joy of the reunion with the Beloved in their souls, and enjoy the counted days of their stay in this world like those waiting patiently for the time to break their fast… and enjoy the delight of a thousand experiences within one.

Along with the eagerness and joy of seeing the Eternal Sultan, the servant takes great delight in being under divine supervision; thus the pettiest action for His sake is fulfilled in a joy of worship.

Presented here is a humble window opened to the noble Prophet's blessed sayings; the actual scope of these profoundly concise statements can never be fully captured nor contained in volumes of similar attempts.

عَنْ جُنْدَبِ بْنِ عَبْدِ اللهِ الْبَجَلِيّ قَالَ قَالَ رَسُولُ اللهِ صَلَّى اللهُ عَلَيْهِ وَسَلَّمَ:

اقْرَءُوا الْقُرْآنَ مَا ائْتَلَفَتْ عَلَيْهِ قُلُوبُكُمْ فَإِذَا اخْتَلَفْتُمْ فَقُومُوا عَنْهُ

RESONANCE WITH THE QUR'AN

*"Read the Qur'an as long as your hearts are in accord; when
you are in discord, stop reading it."*

(Bukhari, Fadail al-Qur'an, 37; Muslim, Ilm, 3)

This hadith can be understood in two different ways. Firstly, irrespective of an act as meritorious as that of reading the Qur'an or other similar acts of worship, after a certain period of engagement a sense of weariness may dawn on the heart, the soul, our senses and other faculties. Carrying on in spite of such signs of weariness may cause the heart to be detached and lose focus from the act in point.

Although the Companions of the Prophet Muhammad (peace and blessings be upon him) both intensively and extensively engaged in various forms of worship, nonetheless they would seek ways to further expand on the ever rising threshold and would explore various methods in order to achieve that. Some of them, for example, would spend the entire night in prayer and vigilance with ropes tying themselves in the mosque, so that sleep could be resisted. Numerous others would try to keep an ascetic way of living by dramatically restraining their eating, drinking, and sleeping habits. Perhaps based on such rich legacies and the belief to dwell and be driven by one's innate spiritual strength beyond the physical shackles continues to inspire people in our contemporary times, where they try to live a life of asceticism; even though, with hope, they may well be rewarded for their sincere intentions, nevertheless one needs to be free from fatigue in order to qualitatively maximize the benefit in their worship.

Although, the depth in one's relationship with the Infinite One is an inestimable and unquenchable journey, nevertheless, when applied over a certain period of time, just like the muscles in our bodies can get tired so do the spiritual mechanisms and faculties within us. As a result, when those engaged in devotional acts, do not give themselves a required level of rest, loss of concentration and preoccupation of the mind with mundane thoughts instead of sublime feelings, emerges. Introducing a combination of different forms of positive activities can be stimulating to mind and focus. For example, if one feels wearied by voluntary *salah* or prayers, reading materials that enlightens the mind and affords a sense of wonderment about elevated realities can engage the mind comfortably as new information fed to the mind excites its functionalities. This can be followed by some meditating and recitation of some prayers for that spiritual supplement. Focus back to one's assigned studies after that can be all be the required variable which not only feeds the mind and spirit its share but also productively and efficiently utilizes time.

Monotony and stagnation is not part of nature, from the colorful changes of seasons to the multiplicity and diversity in creation across the earth, it appears as if everything, besides their multiple usefulness and purposes, is designed for the admiring gazes and insights of the human person. Variation and positive lifestyles should therefore also be part of our lives in general and part of our worship in particular, since human beings are considered to be the miniature universe, our design reflects that reality. The following verse quite succinctly gives this advice honest and in sync with the need for variation in human nature:

> "*Therefore, when you are free (from one task), resume (another task)...*" (In-shirah 94:7).

On a different note, there can also be a second inference drawn from the above-mentioned hadith as if to say: "*read the Qur'an as long as you keep up the unity, attachment, and agreement between your hearts.*" It is a very bitter reality that from time to time the verses of the Qur'an have been abused as deficient interpretations been taken as absolute. This goes back as early as the first century after the holy Prophet passed away.

History has witnessed the struggle between particular mindsets who attempted to darken the light of the Qur'an. Although they may have been sincere in their approach, nonetheless the *Kharijites* can be considered as the first who introduced literalism in Islam. They would argue that *"the truth is whatever the Qur'an is saying word for word."* Even though this sentence does bear truth nonetheless *Kharijites* neither took the Prophet's interpretation on the issue at hand, nor did they consider the Companions' different approaches and they also did not take the commentaries of the scholars, who had excellent command of Arabic language into consideration. Its outcome drove hearts towards disagreement and division. Furthermore, in defense to their position, some of those who adopted the literal approach abused Qur'anic meanings in such a way that suited their held views and would use them against those who disagreed with them. This also caused more disagreement and fragmentation within the community; especially at a sensitive time when "winning hearts" was much more urgently needed then winning over debate for the sake of it.

To come to an end, at the time, although every one would use the Qur'an as their point of reference yet rather then exploring deeper understandings, those with literal approach gave preference to take an immediate and superficial methodology which reduced the sophistication and therefore the intent of the religion towards blind alleyways. Our contemporary times are not an exception to that drift, for literalism and therefore reductionism continues its rudiments. Human ego by nature seeks approval and self-righteousness and sometimes in order to prove our point of view, we take that subjective approach and use Qur'anic references to support our ideas within the framework of our relative understandings and make that interpretation the guide.

The gravity of the matter should be realized and refrain exercised. Otherwise, in pursuit to guard our constructed point of view, we may not only discomfort but deeply disadvantage people from true access and awareness of the depth and breadth of this Noble Qur'an.

Against this backdrop then it is most befitting to interpret that reading the Qur'an in such a manner and with such intention and approaches discussed above does not and will not unite believers' heart with Qur'an as the center, rather, it will cause discord and dissention.

عَنْ أَبِي هُرَيْرَةَ قَالَ قَالَ رَسُولُ اللهِ صَلَّى اللهُ عَلَيْهِ وَسَلَّمَ:

أَكْمَلُ الْمُؤْمِنِينَ إِيمَانًا أَحْسَنُهُمْ خُلُقًا وَخِيَارُكُمْ خِيَارُكُمْ لِنِسَائِهِمْ خُلُقًا

36

A WOMAN IS ONE HALF OF A WHOLE

*"The most excellent among you in faith, is the most virtuous of you;
and the most virtuous of you is the one who treats his wife best."*

(Tirmidhi, Rada, 11; Darimi, Riqaq, 74)

To keep up and honor the moral code outlined in the principles of Islam, exalts a person to such otherwise unattainable peaks, to such elevated states that no other act of worship can in comparison, achieve that.

It is quite an unfortunate reality but women continue to be mistreated and deemed as secondary citizens in many parts of the world, perhaps even in those circles where they advocate and endorse women's rights. On the contrary, according to Qur'anic principles and many hadith women are viewed to be one half of a whole. We believe that when two halves come together, the true unity of a human person emerges. If this unity does not exist, humanity does not exist. Man and woman complement one another, for each finds in the other one's own true value; this is given so that the Divine principles are abided by in balance is not abused against that balance.

116

In addition to the literatures and many anecdotes, the gentle Prophet was gracious towards women and always encouraged others to do the same. Since he was directed by Revelation, he did not need any one's advice, He would consult with his wives on range of different matters and issues and set precedents for his followers. He taught his nation Muslim men were to give their women every consideration. This was quite a radical approach in his time when not just in the Arabian peninsula but all over the world women were grossly mistreated and taken advantage of. While in some parts of the world, burial of first-born baby girls alive was the norm, in other parts, the question whether women even had a soul were disputed, yet in other areas forced marriages and certainly no access to education were imposed upon girls. In such times, viewing women with respect and to consider them to be equal participants in society were revolutionary on all accounts. He began teaching his people through his own relationship with his wives.

For example, the conditions laid down in the Treaty of Hudaybiya disappointed many Muslims, for one of the conditions stipulated that pilgrimage is not to be conducted that year. The Messenger of God ordered them to sacrifice their animals and take off their pilgrim attire. Some Companions hesitated, hoping that he would change his mind. Noticing this reluctance, the Prophet returned to his tent and consulted his wife Umm Salama what she thought of the situation. In doing this, he taught Muslim men to always exchange ideas with women on important and for that matter on any and all kinds of matters. The Prophet's blessed tradition introduced, secured the honored dignity of women that had been trampled and held in contempt, women attained elevated status in both worlds.

Without discrimination both men and women acquired a sublime essence, as God declares in the Qur'an: *"Surely We have created human of the best stature as the perfect pattern of creation"* (Tin 95:4). Here *insan* (human) refers to both men and women together. Human beings, irrespective of their genders were created as an index of the universe.

With the eye of imagination and in fact if it were possible, one could travel through the macrocosms and inspected the majestic nebulas and illuminating stars, then returned to the microcosmic realm and journeyed through the world of particles in seamless motions, the harmonious orbit of electrons and protons around a nucleus; if the entire cosmos were to be journeyed through and their marvel were to be witnessed, one would still not be able to find anything even comparable to the comprehensibility and the sophistication of the human being; not just on the account of their physical compositions, but in regard to the uniqueness of their spiritual and intellectual faculties, truly humanity is designed as par excellence, "in the best of pattern" as the Giver of Form and Patterns declares in His Divine Speech.

God created human beings like a miniature book that contains within it relations with all worlds of existence, just like the index. Many realms are concealed within this compact being. Human beings may consider themselves minuscule creatures in comparison to all that there is; however they are unaware of the immense potential latent within them. This fact is most beautifully expressed by the Caliph Ali ibn Abu Talib; *"You consider yourself to be a mere small object. However, all the abodes of existence, all the worlds are contained in you."*

As a matter of fact, human is an index of the universe. Only the one who with correct insight surveys reads the universe can marvel at the truth of the human design. Whereas a traveler whose gazes are fixated at the outer realities and have perceives entities as particulars without recognizing the unity within them all, could potentially search the entire universe but will not be able to perceive those subtle meanings neither will they attain full awareness of the mystery and truth that lies in human nature. The Elevator Himself explicitly reveals that, *"Surely We have created human of the best stature as the perfect pattern of creation."* Every tread that occurs in the universe is marked within human beings.[16]

The Creator reveals in the Qur'an, *"We have honored the children of Adam"* (Isra 17:70). And amongst many other similar verses, God sets quite explicitly the criterion for superiority as He declares: *"O Humankind, We have created you of a single pair of men and women and made you into nations and tribes so that you may get to know each other (not that you may despise each other). Verily in the sight of God, the most honored amongst you is the most righteous of you. God is full aware of all"* (49:13)

The above verse directly and explicitly exalts humanity, regardless of gender, race, color and most interestingly to note, even regardless their belief. For 'the most honored in the sight of God' is the "one righteous in the heart." Not the man or the woman, neither the black nor the white amongst us. This honor and title accorded by God Himself elevates human beings to levels which no other worldly titles can match.

---

[16]   It is not in the scope of this particular volume of work to elaborate on the mystery of the human nature and their exaltedness as well as their relatedness to creation at large. Books have been written on the subject matter and we warmly refer you to those.

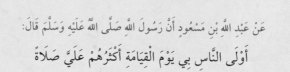

عَنْ عَبْدِ اللهِ بْنِ مَسْعُودٍ أَنَّ رَسُولَ اللهِ صَلَّى اللهُ عَلَيْهِ وَسَلَّمَ قَالَ:

أَوْلَى النَّاسِ بِي يَوْمَ الْقِيَامَةِ أَكْثَرُهُمْ عَلَيَّ صَلَاةً

⟨37⟩

SIGNIFICANCE OF INVOKING BLESSINGS ON THE PROPHET

*"The one nearest to me on the Day of Judgment is the one
who invokes blessings on me the most."*

(Tirmidhi, Salat, 357)

As it is mentioned in many other hadith, the importance of invoking peace and blessings on the Prophet is established above all by the Qur'an:

Surely God and His angels bless the Prophet. O you who believe, invoke the blessings of Allah on him, and pray to God to bestow His peace on him, greeting him with the best greeting.

If the Almighty already grants blessings and peace to the Prophet, one may wonder what the wisdom could be for the believers to do the same. The ensuing discussion will attempt to answer this mystery.

The essence of all the good deeds, prosperity and Divine blessing, is Prophet Muhammad, peace and blessings be upon him. He is the unfailing, unerring guide, the archetype to be taken as a model by all, and it is the holy Prophet who leads to the Path of Balance, who has established the most beautiful and most comprehensible mode to serve the Only One Worthy of servitude and who has therefore ushered a new era that enables human beings to potentially live to the peak of their humanity.

He is the means, selected by God, to lead people out of darkness towards light. He will accordingly be granted the equal amount of reward for every good deed earned by his followers. In accordance with the principle *one who causes is like the doer*" (Muslim, Imara, 133), the same amount of reward for every good and righteous deeds done by those who follow this Model of Goodness, will continue to be recorded in his book of good deeds until the Day of Judgment.

To the Prophet belongs *Maqam al-Mahmud*, the esteemed position or rank assigned to him as the intercessor in the Day of Judgment. His book of reward did not close at his death. Rather, as he continues to accumulate the good works and pious deeds, his rank will continue to increase to ever higher levels, and resultantly the breadth of his intercession will expand even further (Bukhari, Adhan, 8). And with God's will, the holy Prophet will have a right to intercede for greater numbers and masses of those who followed him.

With this backdrop let us now look at this question from two different angles. Firstly, by invoking peace and blessings on the Messenger of God, we renew our oath to him as the Prophet and express our desire to be part of his community. We utter 'peace and blessings be upon him' as if to signify our plea: "O Prophet we remembered and thought of you as our Prophet and with each remembrance prayed to God to increase your worth and degree so that we too could join and be related to you." Since our prayer is made with the conviction that God will ever increase the esteem of the *Owner of Maqam al-Mahmud*, the sphere of his intercession will expand and will consequently increase the probability of number of those who can benefit from his intercession on the Day of Judgment.

Secondly, one's prayer to God for the elevation of the Prophet's rank will act as a means to bring one in the sphere of his intercession. It is actually we, not the noble Prophet, who is in constant need to invoke Divine blessings and peace upon him. In this process, each such utterance acknowledges the Prophethood of Prophet Muhammad, peace and blessings be upon him, signifying his eminence; at the same time in comparison we realize our smallness, our nothingness and our dire need to belong to his community. Just as someone would rely upon their state of which they maybe a citizen of to come to their aid in times of need or danger; so do we stand in need, on account of our incompetence, poverty, and the anxiety, from the terrible Day of Reckoning – it is possible to feel the stun of that Day – wherein the dire need to seek intercession from the Prophet will be every heart's hunt. Through our invocations now we inform him of our present state and petition our plead to be remembered then.

May The Granter of Honor, privilege us with the intercession of His Prophet, the one who has by His leave, the widest dispensation to intercede in that Supreme Tribunal in our favor.

It is worthy to reflect on the good news that God offered special gifts to every Prophet, an exclusive something that they may pass on to their followers. When the other Prophets were granted the right to ask for something for their peoples, they all requested benefit their followers in this realm of test, this world. When the same opportunity to request was offered to Prophet Muhammad, peace and blessings be upon him, his response: *"I left what I would give to my people to the Hereafter … and that is my intercession"* (Bukhari, Tafsir al-Sura, (17) 5, Tayammum, 1).

121

عَنْ عُرْوَةَ بْنِ الزُّبَيْرِ أَنَّ حَكِيمَ بْنَ حِزَامٍ أَخْبَرَهُ أَنَّهُ قَالَ لِرَسُولِ اللهِ صَلَّى اللهُ

عَلَيْهِ وَسَلَّمَ أَرَأَيْتَ أُمُورًا كُنْتُ أَتَحَنَّثُ بِهَا فِي الْجَاهِلِيَّةِ هَلْ لِي فِيهَا مِنْ شَيْءٍ

فَقَالَ لَهُ رَسُولُ اللهِ صَلَّى اللهُ عَلَيْهِ وَسَلَّمَ:

أَسْلَمْتَ عَلَى مَا أَسْلَفْتَ مِنْ خَيْرٍ وَالتَّحَنُّثُ التَّعَبُّدُ

THE AGE OF IGNORANCE—CHARITY AND GOOD DEEDS

In response to a question from one Companion regarding whether or not there was reward for charity and good deeds made during the Age of Ignorance, the Prophet said, "How do you think you became a Muslim?"

(Muslim, Iman, 194)

I do not know if there was the concept of a taxation system or charity in the Age of Ignorance, but one of the most important themes that stand out through the poetical legacies from that time is generosity. Behaving generously, meant spending from one's wealth when necessary. This important dynamic later was employed in Islam. It went beyond necessity and meant to spend freely in God's way - in the second verse of Qur'an it states, *"and out of what We have provided for them, they spend…"* (Baqara 2:3).

If those people did what they did on the path of good or for His sake, they can each be a source of hope. From spending in charity to maintaining justice, goodness is always goodness. For example, before the advent of Islam a Yemeni merchant delivered goods to an influential Meccan, who later refused to pay. The wronged man cried out for justice and a league called the *hilf al-fudul* (Allegiance of the Virtuous) was formed to deliver justice. The future Prophet to be was a party to this league, for the sake of goodness on its own merit.

Similarly after prophethood he commended that act and said, *"Under similar circumstances I would act the same way and be a part of them."* Also when the Ka'ba was being restored he carried rocks for the sake in order to contribute for what was an act of righteousness would help those who were making repairs. In the later years on he favorably mentioned this.

In this respect, regardless the time period, whether it be during the Age of Ignorance or the when Islam had entered, every act of goodness made towards humanity is good. Goodness on itsd own merit is good. Any and every good deed made to others leads to new added good deeds, on one hand, and acts as a protection from evil, on the other.

As stated in one of our holy Prophet's hadith, once upon a time, three people were locked up in a cave by a big rock. They prayed to God for deliverance, and each mentioned a good work that they had sincerely done for His sake. Eventually The Preserver accepted their prayers and caused the rock to be removed. The difficulties they bore in the cave were grueling for the ego, but that one day those challenges became the very means for the rock to roll away. In proportion to the quality and quantity, the acts of goodness in this world that caused that huge rock to roll away can also disperse the defiant rocks that can fall on the path towards Heaven. If God wills, they can also become a bridge crossing believers over hell, or even a shuttle that takes one directly to Heaven.

Of course good deeds are not restricted to be done for the believers only, for goodness to anyone is goodness, irrespective of one's outlooks. Perhaps due to it being one of the pillars of faith, Zakat[17] is an exception to this, feeding the poor in general when giving charity had no reservations. Goodness and charity goes beyond the human realm, to take care of animals and trees

---

[17] During the caliphate of Umar ibn Abdul Aziz, zakat money circulated towns for the rightful recipients but since there was no one, the money was transferred to the poor among the neighboring Christians and Jews.

are also considered worthy of reward. In fact, to take account of numerous hadith and the general spirit of religion, the protection of the entire earth and its ecological balance is meritorious acts to the point of obligations. To live in a safe and green environment and then to conserve it in that balance onto the next generation is the ecology's right upon us.

All deeds of goodness in relation to the time when done will be recorded in one's book of good deeds. In respect to the future, these good deeds can become the shield which will prevent one from falling into error; they dry up the roots of evil and instead nourish and develop goodness and overtime make it easier to perform good deeds, to the point that it becomes second nature to the doer of good deeds.

On this backdrop, even during the Age of Ignorance when these good acts were performed without the consciousness of God and if they were prolific like our Prophet said, they can became the means for a person to enter Islam, similarly then when a believer does the acts of righteousness, then one act can equal to thousand and thousands to countless numbers and they become a shield against possible future dangers.

How can one reconcile when a doer of good acts are not always become protected and sometimes do make falls, how for example, in some sound hadiths, it mentions devils to be chained during the month of Ramadan, yet we still witness great mischief during Ramadan. How for example God says that no harm will come to those when performing the *tawaf* (circumambulation around the Ka'ba), which is a very sacred act and is believed that one is in God's view, a position envied by so many believers, yet despite all this some are kicked and thousands are trampled under foot. How should such apparent paradoxes be understood? What this indicates is a very subtle point for devil does not bother with those who have no regard for spiritual quests and no belief in God. However, those who go to mosques, who serve religion at a time when it has become very difficult to do, it is those whose lives' aim is to earn God's pleasure and avoid malice who face strong challenges and obstacles. In this respect it can be said that if the devil were not chained during Ramadan, people could never escape from evil. At the same time, if people can walk on Heaven's path in spite of all the hardships, then their good deeds are that vehicle for they do not get into much harm before those enemies and their attacks. In other words, these people they are so focused to serve Islam under heavy conditions that God will protect them and turn their good works into lightning rods against harm.

124

عَنْ أَبِي هُرَيْرَةَ عَنِ النَّبِيِّ صَلَى اللهُ عَلَيْهِ وَسَلَّمَ يُرْوَي عَنْ رَبِّهِ جَلَّ وَعَلَا قَالَ :
وَعِزَّتِي لَا أَجْمَعُ عَلَى عَبْدِي خَوْفَيْنِ وَأَمْنَيْنِ إِذَا خَافَنِي فِي الدُّنْيَا
أَمَّنْتُهُ يَوْمَ الْقِيَامَةِ وَإِذَا أَمَّنَنِي فِي الدُّنْيَا أَخَفْتُهُ يَوْمَ الْقِيَامَةِ

(39)

TWO TRUSTS AND TWO FEARS

*Question: While according to an authentic hadith, it is said that
God does not grant two trusts or fears to His servants at the
same time, in reality, we are leading very comfortable and even
luxurious lives. How can these two facts be reconciled?*

(Sahih Ibn Hibban, 2:406; Kanz al-Ummal, 3:709)

Fear (*khawf*) and hope (*raja'*) are two bounties granted or to be granted by Almighty God to human beings. The ability to internalize these two Divine bounties in a measured manner while trying to reach God is another, and arguably, greater bounty. The noble translation of the hadith referred to in the question is as follows: *"I will not give my servant two trusts at the same time; I will not give him two fears at the same time."*

125

This question carries an assumption. There is an implied association between one's sense of security and life of comfort and possibly luxury, while fear is interpreted as leading a life with poverty and destitution. At first glance, this may readily provide a partial explanation, but it would be wrong to assume that this is an exhaustive commentary on the hadith. Another way to understand this hadith could be as follows:

"I will not grant two trusts to My servant at the same time.." This hadith could mean that for those who lead a life aimed at this world, without concern for what lies beyond, for those who neglect and abandon their spiritual faculties to the point of total decay and death, rather choosing to live in oblivion of the revelation, there will be no security for the Hereafter. Their hearts will be in constant anguish about what is to come.

On the other hand, God also does not grant *"... two fears at the same time."* If individuals live in this world with awe and a sense of constant concern, and if they say or are able to say, either in their words or behavior: *"O My Lord! Without Your beneficence, I cannot protect my faith. Without Your favor, I cannot maintain my spirituality. Without Your Generosity, I cannot survive. Without Your mercy and compassion, I cannot be admitted to Paradise. Indeed, without Your Beloved Prophet, who is Mercy is for All the Worlds, I would never be guided to the straight path and would be misguided forever,"* and if they constantly check themselves with such concerns, using every opportunity for self-renewal, then, with the will of God, they may not fear that which could be a terrible horror for some, the Hereafter.

Although the hadith does not directly allude to worldly possessions, nonetheless believers who lead a life of ease and comfort have a lesson to learn from it as well.

If people act as if they were born to lead a life that focuses only on this world, and when they have no fears or concerns for the Hereafter, then they should be deeply concerned about themselves and what may be impending.

Even if there is a level of realization and some degree of concern for the Hereafter, individuals should be wary of the ease and comfort they may be experiencing. According to authentic narrations, Umar ibn Abd al-Aziz would recite the Qur'anic verse, *"You consumed in your worldly life your (share of) pure, wholesome things, and enjoyed them fully (without considering the due of the Hereafter, and so have taken in the world the reward of all your good deeds)"* (Ahqaf 46:20) repeatedly until he would be utterly exhausted; even a believer as pious as Umar ibn Abd al-Aziz was deeply concerned about the possibility of remaining empty-handed in the Hereafter.

It is quite normal for a believer with a sound heart to entertain such levels of deep concern, and as a matter of fact, this sense of awe is actually the relative outcome of profound reflections. The Most Generous One had granted substantial wealth to Abdurrahman ibn Awf and Uthman ibn Affan, two of the esteemed Companions of Prophet Muhammad, peace be upon him; He may grant the same to any one of us. In that case, believers should make use of their wealth for the sake of purposes higher than themselves and serve humanity for the sake of God. It is not necessary to give away possessions entirely; it is better to give in measured terms to those who are in need. A part of the assets should be retained so that they can be invested and wealth multiplied; thus, in the end one can donate a greater amount.

This should be a benchmark against which we frequently check the level of our hearts. Can we comfortably say, deep within our consciences, that we are ready to give every time we hear the command and suggestions by Our Lord? Can we say, *"Yes, O My Lord, I am ready to give!"*? If we can do this, in other words, if the state of our heart is not attached to the possessions we have, then an increase in wealth can bear no negative impact upon us, and their property will not be the cause of any worry concerning the Hereafter, if God so wills. On the other hand, if a person insists on living heedlessly, having no belief or spiritual quest, simply, yet unwisely seeking to please the never-pleased carnal self—may God forbid—such a person will be bogged down in the swamp, headfirst. Let these two points not be confused.

عَنْ عَبْدِ الرَّحْمَنِ بْنِ أَبِي بَكْرَةَ عَنْ أَبِيهِ قَالَ أَثْنَى رَجُلٌ عَلَى رَجُلٍ عِنْدَ النَّبِيِّ صَلَّى اللّٰهُ عَلَيْهِ وَسَلَّمَ فَقَالَ:

وَيْلَكَ قَطَعْتَ عُنُقَ صَاحِبِكَ قَطَعْتَ عُنُقَ صَاحِبِكَ مِرَارًا ثُمَّ قَالَ:

مَنْ كَانَ مِنْكُمْ مَادِحًا أَخَاهُ لَا مَحَالَةَ فَلْيَقُلْ أَحْسِبُ فُلَانًا وَاللّٰهُ حَسِيبُهُ وَلَا

أُزَكِّي عَلَى اللّٰهِ أَحَدًا أَحْسِبُهُ كَذَا وَكَذَا إِنْ كَانَ يَعْلَمُ ذَلِكَ مِنْهُ

(40)

THE ESSENCE & BALANCE OF PRAISE AND APPLAUSE

*A man praised another man in front of the Prophet. The noble Prophet
said to him, "Woe to you, you have smitten your friend's neck," repeating
it several times and then added, "Whoever among you has to praise his
brother should say, 'I think that he is so and so, and God knows exactly
the truth, and I do not confirm anybody's good conduct before God, but I
think him so and so,' if he really knows what he says about him."*

(Bukhari, Shahada, 16)

The issue of praising others in their face deserves a lot of attention;
however we will examine one or two important aspects. Firstly
we will discuss praising a person before the Creator and secondly,

then we will discuss how such praise impacts and even spiritually kills the person who is hears his own praise.

Words that praise, admire or honor a person should be chosen carefully. Otherwise that person applauding will "smite his neck" of the one applauded as the hadith indicates. Additionally, the Prophet stated that he could not praise anyone before God, and I think this undoubtedly provides us with a strong point of reference. The Prophet set the standard for us to follow when he himself repeatedly emphasized not to give preference to him above Prophet Moses or Jonah. Therefore a true believer should always strive for humbleness and unassuming nature amongst people. One, who draws on this principle, will be able to desist from expectations, anticipation of courtesy from others, the quest for high rank positions and will be able to stay away from flattery and hypocrisy.

On another note, it is reported that the Prophet stated that the extensive grieving and cry of close ones will bring suffering to the deceased. There are two opinions on this narration. The Prophet's wife Aisha based on two verses from the Qur'an where it is mentioned that no one will be burdened with the crime/mistake of someone else, questioned the validity of the hadith as being a true record. However scholars have reached consensus on the authenticity of this hadith and have elucidated that the dead will be disturbed if the grieving loved lament for them and in the process may utter things that maybe contrary to the principle of God's oneness, His decree and power.

In conclusion, if someone is praised, who has yet not reached the level of spiritual maturity when they are able to grasp the essence of the praise and reject any imaginary ranks that may come with it; the praise will be only to their detriment. Who knows, maybe (...) was such a person. Because of the exaggerated praise from the people around him, he actually started to believe that he was the *Mujaddid*, than the *Mahdi* and in the end the *Messiah* and ultimately strayed from the true path.

Now perhaps there are more confused people. Recently my friends informed me that there were 15-20 individuals in Turkey who have proclaimed that they are the *Mahdi*. I assume that they lost their way in a similar way.

Since we are talking about praise and its danger, I would like to remind my friends who compete in servitude to the Creator and as a result are constantly complimented, of the following. The most selfless, devout and suffering person of our time ignored his accomplishment in terms of service and stated that he was only contributing to establish a foundation on which following generations can serve Allah and humanity. He scolded his carnal self (*nafs*) and warned it not to be vain. He said: "*Oh my insincere soul don't be complacent about your servitude to this religion. Allah sometimes lets a lost soul carry the torch for supporting and complementing his religion.*" Since we cannot consider ourselves of the purified ones but rather the ones who are stray, we should regard our servitude and observance as a gratitude for all our past and present blessings, a natural duty, and obligation. By doing so, we will finally refrain from arrogance and insincerity.

Bubbles on the surface of water shine as they reflect the rays of the sun. When it is dark or they do not face the sun their ability to radiate the light is diminished and they are mere bubbles. Its virtue lies in its reflection of the sunlight, but it could never be the sun. Just as the bubbles on the water, if you are capable of reflecting whatever comes from God, you are among the fortunate ones. Our approach is straightforward. Greatest obligation and duty is to serve God. We do not crave for praise and or ranks that may follow, from. We desire to be "*one among the many*" as Ali ibn Abu Talib stated. Believing hearts find their greatness in the group and a collective conscience.

Immortal truth cannot be based on mortal individuals. If we do so, ideals will expire with the death of these individuals. A strong relationship and spiritual unity with one another must always be maintained. We need to reach the spiritual level where we are able to negate ourselves, for humility is a sign of greatness and arrogance a sign of small character.

Saying "*I did it ... it is my accomplishment*" is a form of blasphemy as it worships the ego. Ego needs to be transcended and we must show 'us' to the Divine. In addition to avoid from controversy and refrain from even the smallest of lies is among our duties. As I have mentioned on previous occasions, our individual capacity is insignificant; it is the collective spiritual level that counts. Consequently, praise and applause should not sweep us off our feet or keep us from fulfilling our duties. This can be accomplished only through adherence to the above-mentioned principles.